GREG BOTTRILL
STEPHANIE COOK

Love Letters to PLAY.

CORWIN

A SAGE Publishing Company

A SAGE company
2455 Teller Road
Thousand Oaks, California 91320
(0800)233-9936
www.corwin.com

SAGE Publications Ltd
1 Oliver's Yard
55 City Road
London EC1Y 1SP

SAGE Publications India Pvt Ltd
B 1/I 1 Mohan Cooperative Industrial Area
Mathura Road
New Delhi 110 044

SAGE Publications Asia-Pacific Pte Ltd
3 Church Street
#10-04 Samsung Hub
Singapore 049483

© 2022 Greg Bottrill and Stephanie Cook

First edition published in 2022

Editor: Amy Thornton
Senior project editor: Chris Marke
Cover design: Wendy Scott
Typeset by: C&M Digitals (P) Ltd, Chennai, India
Printed in the UK

Library of Congress Control Number: 2022939149

British Library Cataloguing in Publication Data

A catalogue record for this book is available from the British Library.

ISBN 978-1-5296-0801-4
ISBN 978-1-5296-0800-7 (pbk)

At SAGE we take sustainability seriously. Most of our products are printed in the UK using responsibly sourced papers and boards. When we print overseas we ensure sustainable papers are used as measured by the PREPS grading system. We undertake an annual audit to monitor our sustainability.

Contents

About the authors   v

Preface   vii

How to read Love Letters to Play   ix

What each Love Letter *might offer you*   xi

Part 1 Love letters to play   1

Part 2 Other love letters to play   203

Part 3 The green and black books   209

About the authors

Greg Bottrill

Greg is passionate about play and believes that play is who we are - it is in our DNA. Having taught in both KS2 and Early Years, his experiences have taken him on an adventure into childhood itself, galvanising his belief that education must be something done with children, not to them. He hopes that the pages of this book will support you to write your own Love Letter to play, so that you can share it with whoever will listen. It's time...

Stephanie Cook

Stephanie is an Early Years and Key Stage 1 teacher who is passionate about children's freedoms, their right to be seen as equals within society, and the powerful possibilities of play. She believes that education should be centred around childhood's intrinsic motivation to learn through play-fullness and an authentic re-connection with Nature. Much of her thinking also explores 'alternative' educational approaches and how these might bring positive change to the English education system.

Play loves you.

Unconditionally, passionately, completely.

It loved you from the moment you were born with all its big glowing heart.

Play had so many gifts for you. It gave them freely, it gave them because it cared for every atom of you.

Every day, play told you of its love for you. It reached out its hand to take. Play wanted to hold you in its warm embrace. It sang for you.

Once upon a time, you were in love with play too. You wanted to spend every waking hour in its company, and you joined in with its song.

Play showed you how to marvel. It taught you, it showed you how to dream, and it revealed your ability to have communion with the world of animals and trees, rivers and the seas.

And since play had such great and deep love for you, because its care for you was so fathomless, it was able to offer the same love to all. Its love could not be contained or controlled.

For it was a wild love - it was in you and me and everyone. Play showed all of us its tenderness, its courage, and its strength. In fact, its love was so strong that it became us. It was almost impossible to see where we ended and where play began.

Together we formed a love like no other.

But where is play now? Where is its love within our days, and in the childhoods we see before us today? Are children immersed in its rich-ness, are they recipients of its love?

Or have we turned our back upon play? Have we made ourselves brittle and hard-hearted? Do we feel anything at all for play or have we con-signed it to a life of unrequited love, abandoned and bereft?

Or perhaps its song still echoes inside our chests? Do we remember the love that play showed to us and are we passing its gift to childhood before us as it unfolds into the world? Do our hearts beat with love for play?

Only we have the answers to these questions and all the others that we will discover within the pages of this book.

For 'Love Letters to Play' - like play itself - is a question. It is asking you what you feel, what you hold deep within you. Play needs your love like never before since it is in peril of becoming a lost word. It is our hope that as you read this book and answer to play with your very being, you will embrace it even more lovingly, even more passionately.

And if the answers we give to the Love Letters are typecast, are the hand-me-downs of what we have been told to be, are the stale narratives of The Economy, of the watchdogs, of those that would entomb the creativity and curiosity of childhood, then perhaps we need the Love Letters even more. Perhaps we are in need of more play, not less.

Because play is trying to talk to us every day - it understands our fear. It knows that we are lost but it will wait for us patiently.

And why?

Because play still loves us. It always, always has and it always, always will…

Greg and Steph

How to read *Love Letters to Play*

As with any book, you are welcome to read *Love Letters to Play* however you wish, but we feel that the best way to get the most from its pages is to dip into it, one page at a time like a pocket, letting each one sit with you for a while, allowing each sentence to rest inside you.

We believe that play, parenting and education need more feeling and soul within them – we need to open ourselves up to who we are, our values and the lens we look through at childhood. So *Love Letters to Play* has been created to immerse you in how it feels to be in love with play, to spark or jolt you, to give you fortitude or open up a new doorway.

Each Love Letter, each hand-written note, has been crafted to suggest, to question and to stir something within you. They are not answers. They are not theory. They are not telling you what to do. You won't find photos of activities that you can copy or explicit ideas for what to do in your days with children.

We hope the pages offer comfort, challenge and the sense that if you are play-full, then you are extraordinary because you have begun the adventure into the redemptive power of play and are treading a pathway towards change within a world that so desperately needs it.

In each Love Letter, you'll discover a question in bold. This has been done to provide a starting point for thinking or discussions. If you are reading this book as a group or as part of a study course, then we hope the book is like a landscape for you to explore together and opens up debate and further questioning.

If you are reading it by yourself, then we hope that *Love Letters to Play* shows itself as a companion to turn to and offers you solace or prompts to quietly consider.

In effect, the Love Letters are about you and who you are. We might even say that you write your own love letter to play every day you offer it to childhood and make its heart sing with choice and creativity, with its communion with the world.

However, if you know deep in your heart that play's love is unrequited, then perhaps today might be the day to pick up the pen and begin once more. Play loves you and with each love letter you write, its love will burn brighter, and maybe then you might just feel alive once more …

What each Love Letter might offer you

As you read a Love Letter, the following suggested questions might help you in your reflections:

1. What do I think this Love Letter is showing me about childhood, play and who I am?

2. How does this Love Letter make me feel about childhood, myself, the world I see around me, my time spent with children?

3. What words in this Love Letter mean most to me and how might I begin to use them in my own Love Letter, in my own narrative of play and childhood?

4. What is my heart-felt answer to the question in bold? What do I truly believe?

5. How do I show children what I believe about the bold question? How do I live the answer?

6. What Love Letter to Play of my own will I 'write' today through my actions and the choices I make for children?

7. If I have not 'written' a Love Letter to Play for some time, can I confront myself and ask why? What is preventing me from returning love to play? If what is preventing me is something outside myself, what can I do to question it, to act against it?

You may want to reflect on these questions mentally, or you might want to spend some time free writing your response to each Love Letter.

If you are part of a study course, you could share your responses with one another to create a collective Love Letter. This could be in small groups, taking one word, one question or one Love Letter to consider and respond to.

In some way, each Love Letter is a portal to further thinking around continuous provision, the experiences we offer children in their days, the timetables we structure, the rules we make children follow, the stories we share with them and how, and ultimately to these questions:

When is childhood's adventure ended? Who is responsible for ending it, who gave them the power to do so, and how do we rise against them?

When did we accept that separating children from play was 'good' for children? Why was it allowed to happen?

What is our power to keep play from becoming a lost love?

How do we align ourselves with those who still believe in play and its love for us? How do we plan to nourish one another and bring the change that we know needs to come into the world?

What will you do to act?

Part One

Love Letters to Play

#Play is freedom

Acaronar

A-car-o-nar

CATALAN

(Verb) to tenderly, lovingly pull someone closer

Play is tender.

When was the last time we did something with tenderness?

And is tenderness something children should be shown?

How are we tender with childhood?

If we answer that children should be shown it, then it is telling to look over at the Adult World to see how capable it is of offering tenderness to children.

If we break a day into hourly pockets of time, can we detect even a glimmer of devotion to childhood?

If we can't discover tenderness, then it shows us what does and doesn't lie at the heart of what we do or are told to do.

Perhaps, when we consider tenderness as 'devotion', we finally understand what others want us to bow to and why our own hearts tell us not to …

#Play is choice

Acatalepsy

A-kat-a-lep-si

ENGLISH

(Noun) the impossibility of comprehending the universe; the belief that human knowledge can never be true certainty

Play is story.

Do we have an unyielding claim to knowledge and learning?

Are we here to deliberately diminish childhood's energy, its library of dream and its innate wonder-fullness and do we replace childhood, slowly redacting its story, 'The Tale of What Life Could Be'?

What if we could comprehend a plot other than our own?

If we possess the capability of comprehending the vastness of childhood's universe, that universe which stretches out beyond horizons with its infinite stories of itself, then we understand the power of putting children at the centre. We disentangle from the trap of our own limitations.

If we choose to deny play and rule knowledge and learning, then we do so not out of strength but out of weakness, not out of right but out of failed imagination.

We have no natural rule over childhood – this is play's message to us: to let childhood tell us its story.

#Play is love

Anam Kara

On-um Ka-rah

GAELIC

(Noun) soul friend

Play is motivation.

It is play that opens the adventure outwards for children - it draws them on.

Yet how quickly we create a child/adult divide, seeing children almost as a separate species, not as equal adventurers.

We seem to show children that the expectation to obey and conform reflects their 'goodness', their 'success', their worthiness of love.

How often we instil fear and shame, how little we show childhood its true value or its belonging.

Does shame or 'punishment' fulfil children, engage them and inspire to go further on into the adventure?

Does it make them want to adventure any further with us?

Childhood explores and overcomes its difficulties through play - it is play that truly motivates children to keep going.

But if we exile children from play, what do we replace it with?

We substitute it with suffering and shame, we create a culture that offers few pathways beyond children meeting the adult 'Yes'.

We show children that they must look for our approval, diverting them from the one thing that they should be seeking: the infinite pathways of play …

If play switches off the dark, then do we try to add back to the darkness, or join play's luminosity?

#Play is connection

Aparigraha

A-par-i-gra-ha

SANSKRIT

(Noun) the practice of detachment; to let go of everything that isn't serving you

Play is release.

What serves childhood?

What doesn't serve childhood and are we capable of letting go of it?

To detach ourselves from the archaism and obsolescence of the past is possibly the greatest demand that childhood makes of us.

When children play, they show us who they are.

Conversely, if we prevent them from playing - from choosing, inventing, creating and exploring - if we give them Diminished Days of Do This, Do That, then we show children who we are.

We reveal our need to control - a need that comes from our lack of courage.

Yet if we have faith in children, if we trust in their choices and their dream, we show our strength and our compassion - we unmask ourselves so that children can see who we truly are.

And this is the reason that play is so transformative - it can take us to a place of incredible vulnerability - since to offer play we have to confront ourselves and our own choices.

It is in this place that we not only unearth the authenticity of children, we discover our own …

#Play is natural

Apnapan

Ap-na-pan

HINDI

(Noun) having a quality where you accept people; think of them as your own, take care of the ones you love not for anything in return

Play is observation.

What are all children looking for from the adults around them?

What is it that they are searching for within their play-full adventures?

We can certainly say that one thing is 'meaning'.

Perhaps that is what play is - children's pursuit of meaning, of making sense of the world both around them and within them. Is this why childhood's burning curiosity is so critical to keep aflame?

Is it also why we as adults need to unlearn ourselves, with all our sense of certainty about 'This Is How Things Are And Can Only Be' so that we rediscover our own curiosity, for surely it is somewhere there within us however hidden we have made it or had it made?

And with this curiosity can we not lean in to see what it is that children are truly seeking and find it alongside them?

Maybe this pursuit of meaning has a powerful destination that it can take us to, one that is play's ultimate outcome - belonging and acceptance - acceptance of who we are and who we are not, of who we are now and who we will become - we belong in play, it is home.

It's time to light the fire in its hearth …

#Play is a portal

Aspaldiko

As-pal-deko

BASQUE

(Noun) the feeling of euphoria when catching up with someone who you haven't seen in a long time

Play is transformation.

Perhaps play offers children the possibility of ascent or, even greater still, a transcendence.

When childhood's imagination is brought to life, it has a seismic capacity to lift children from being in a 'world-that-is-presented-to-them' and move them upwards into 'multiple-worlds-as-can-be-imagined'.

How powerful is this? What alchemical influence play can have on children!

For where we stir imagination, we stir emotion. And where we stir emotion, we create the perfect conditions for enchantment and meaning, purpose and the desire to adventure further.

Maybe this is why we need to imagine better?

Perhaps this is why play has to have greater amplification within the days of childhood? To stir those days vigorously.

What might happen if we had future generations of children who were desperate to learn because they sensed the possibilities within themselves?

What might we discover?

How are we discovering play's possibilities?

And what multiple-worlds-as-can-be-imagined might descend to transform us?

#Play is possibility

Athazagoraphobia

A-tha-zag-or-a-pho-bee-a

ENGLISH

(Noun) the fear of forgetting, being forgotten or ignored, or being replaced

Play is children's way of remembering who they are.

It's like a pattern to return to again and again, the comfort of a storyline to step into at will where they know solace can be found or energy can be expended.

Childhood knows that play exists. It knows that it is 'them'.

If we deny children play, what do we replace it with and, in the moment of replacement, are we substituting who they are with someone who they are not?

And what about the experiences that we substitute play with – what are they?

What comfort, what vitality can be found with them?

Can the same remarkable degree of movement and curiosity, wonder and desire be discovered within them?

Do we offer the same universe of imagination and curiosity when we take play from childhood?

If not, what are we forgetting?

#Play is enigmatic

Ayni

Eye-nee

QUECHUA

(Noun) 'today for you, tomorrow for me', suggesting that giving comes before receiving

Play is bright.

What truly illuminates childhood?

Who brings the most energy into its days - children or the Adult World?

Who possesses the greater imagination and whose heart beats the quickest when immersed in adventure and discovery? And what do we add to the 'today-ism' of childhood?

It's as though play wants to know our motivations, interrogating the history that has brought us to this very moment.

Play demands an answer from us - and how will we respond?

Our answer is given less by what we say but more by what we do.

What gift do we give children?

Days of play that glow with creativity and choice or something else?

#Play is feeling

Bhava

Baa-va

SANSKRIT

(Noun) a mental state of bliss or peace, a oneness that flits into you, especially when you're listening to music

Play is musicality.

What song is play orchestrating within childhood?

Can we hear it when we are in its company?

Perhaps that is why we need to enable play in our adventure - so that the worlds of imagination, fascination, dream and wonder can be heard.

When we were younger, we had a song deep within us, a song of possibility.

Children are now singing it for us, but they also beckon us to join in.

As we listen to the song of play, how will we respond?

Maybe that is play's most powerful question of all - will we sing and how?

#Play is re-imagination

Bilita Mpash

Bil-it-a P-ash

BANTU

(Noun) the opposite of a nightmare - not merely a 'good' dream, but a legendary, blissful state where all is forgiven and forgotten

Play is heart.

Play enables children to create 'legends' of themselves.

It's as though play writes a story of each day that comes, one in which childhood is the central protagonist.

It is critical that we enable children to do this because if we fail to then whose story are they living in?

Can children really adventure inside a day that doesn't belong to them?

Childhood looks to us to give it the conditions of exploration and joy. It wants to feel as though its day belongs to it - choice is at the heart.

Without choice, there is no 'me'. We create the state that children can exist in, so, in a way, their choices lie in the palm of ours. Our choices define the boundaries of theirs.

So perhaps when we see play happening around us - all its rich complexity, its joy and its fascinations - we not only see the legend of childhood, we see the legend also of our own selves …

#Play is adventure

Caim

Cay-m

GAELIC

(Noun) protection; sanctuary; a circle drawn to protect those within it

Play is experimentation.

It is the freedom for children to connect with themselves.

If we remove play, we hinder the powerful potential of childhood's innate ability to learn, to take risks and navigate 'danger' for itself; we remove what is crucial for children - intuition.

And it is this inner voice, this power of hearing with the heart and listening to the soul, that only play can amplify in children.

When we distract children with 'Be careful!' as they play we instil fear, we separate childhood from its instinct to keep itself safe.

How do we permit the world of risk to come back for children?

How do we let their instinctive selves keep safe the playground of the Natural World as they explore and wonder?

What if, as adults, we let children into play's abundant testing ground?

What then?

#Play is enchantment

Cartref

Car-tref

WELSH

(Noun) a place of feeling or belonging; a gathering place for family to join together in laughter and love

Play is togetherness.

What if our settings and classrooms were less about 'learning spaces' and more about 'gathering'; children and loving adults coming together to create a community of play and adventure?

Could this help us imagine the possibilities of childhood?

Can we shift our thinking away from 'education', with all its ghosts of the past that cling on so doggedly, and move closer to a greater focus on co-operation and co-existence?

Aren't all the children before us part of this gathering?

Are there any exceptions to who belongs within it?

Childhood and play say 'No'.

In fact, play, because it is the Great Big Yes, declares that all children are welcome to join together, regardless of how we might view them.

Perhaps if we shared the idea of 'gathering' with children, talked about it as the wonder-full world of which they are a part, they would see even more value within their choices and interactions, they would grow their own sense of co-existence – the gathering of play, of invention, of dreams …

#Play is movement

Chrysalism

Cri-sill-ism

ENGLISH

(Noun) the amniotic tranquility of being indoors during a thunderstorm, listening to waves of rain pattering against the roof while you're nestled inside

Play is security.

To be childhood's harbour, a place to return to, a sanctuary – how does our Time Together with children enable them to know that they are 'seen' and loved?

Do we create the conditions of trust and security within each day?

How does this echo outwards?

If we want an adventure for childhood, if we want the luminosity of play to radiate outwards, then our 'harbour-ism' is an integral part of this – we become a space to which children know they can return and, within the Unknown landscape of play, our presence offers a safety and reassurance.

With each return to us lies the possibility of childhood extending the scope of its adventure ever further – it retreats to then expand outwards with more confidence, more determination, more love in its heart.

Protection then play, nest then adventure, just like every little bird knows and every child should.

#Play is courage

Clairsentient

Clair-sen-tee-ent

ENGLISH

(Noun) someone who feels deeply

Play is passion.

Childhood is full to the brim with its own ideas. It is led by its fascinations.

Perhaps play is asking us to put down What We Want and begin to look for What We Can See. When we do this, we open up the possibility of authentically discovering the children who are before us. We begin to notice children's dreams, what moves them.

Maybe this is what play is trying to show us - that we too can be moved by the world. We might even consider the idea that *it is less about children playing with the world and more about the world playing with children.*

What does play feel like?

And when we unearth the answer can we then begin to feel the same within us too?

Play wants us to feel again - how deeply we will allow it to is reflected in how much play we offer to children in our days.

Is play a barometer of our effervescence?

When we enable play, we are the amplifiers of feeling both in children and ourselves.

When we deny play, we are the lessening.

#Play is hope

Commuovere

Cum-muo-ve-re

LATIN

(Noun) to stir, to touch, to move to tears

Play is emotion.

It's as though play stirs our sensitivity to the world around us.

Through play, we connect, not just to objects, but also to ourselves.

Perhaps that's what happens to us as we pass through childhood and on into the hands of the Adult World – we learn to create two ways of being: one that is born from the struggle to be accepted and validated by adults – an artificial self – and one that quietly sits within us and is brought out when we play.

Through play our real selves emerge.

What do we see as the real self of children?

Is it produced by test, rote, control and function?

And if it's not, then have we confronted ourselves and been moved to think, to hope, to act?

#Play is intrigue

Dadirri

Da-di-ree

NORTHERN TERRITORY ABORIGINAL AUSTRALIAN

(Noun) inner deep listening and awareness; a 'tuning in' experience to deeply understand the beauty of your inner self and the nature around you

Play is re-imagining.

What song is childhood trying to sing to us?

Are we open to not only hearing it, but also joining in with it too? Can we hold our own minds still to grow attentive to what children are revealing in their play?

We can often find ourselves mentally loaded with the anxiety of yesterday or the fear of tomorrow to make space for the Right Now - we find ourselves un-present as though we have tuned out of who we are.

Yet childhood demands our presence - it jolts us to an awakening.

And as we become increasingly play conscious, we begin to see ourselves reflected within the movement and minds of children - we see our own creative selves, our own desire for freedom, for being.

As children play they help us to see ourselves, to come into an understanding of who we are, who we can become.

Can you see yourself reflected in the play around you?

Can you sense yourself?

You're there. Just listen …

#Play is understanding

Datsuzoku

Dat-su-zo-ku

JAPANESE

(Noun) an escape or freedom from the ordinary, a break from daily routine; to discover more creativity and perceive your surroundings with wonder and curiosity

Play is unknowing-ness.

Play is a puzzle, the pieces of which children collect and fit together as they invent, explore and dream.

It's one created from childhood's instinct to encounter, to find out more than meets the eye, and yet it's a puzzle without edge pieces.

With each piece collected, with every discovery, there is something more.

Maybe this is why play is such a force - because it is driven by a curiosity that is inexhaustive, that wants greater understanding, increased risk.

Where play finds an answer it also discovers another question, and another and another.

And with each new question comes more marvel, more invention, more of the Creative Self.

Play is self-perpetuating.

What puzzle do we encounter when children play?

What pieces are we yet to discover and how might we find them?

Perhaps play is less about children's curiosity and more about our own, since if we live within marvel, if we enter the dream of play, we see that we are not just watching the puzzle, we are the puzzle too …

#Play is curiosity

Dauwtrappen

Door-trap-en

DUTCH

(Noun) 'dew treading'; the feeling of walking barefoot on dew-covered morning grass

Play is primal.

It is access to all senses, enabling children to connect with their primal state – the instinctive hunter-gatherer, driven to live and to learn.

If we believe that childhood is sacred, then we must permit it to journey and walk upon the equally sacred surrounding Natural World to be enlightened by its gentle touch.

When we open the door to this world, we allow childhood to experience the cool awakening of Nature's signs.

It's as though, each morning, the world's precious teardrops of dew call on us to let children run free …

What if we freed children from the confines of the walls, the tables, the chairs for a longer period of their lives?

What if we released them from the external drivers of conformity and 'achievement'?

Perhaps if we re-defined success as the re-connection with the very substances that created us – Nature and the raw human connection that flows between us – we might also create a 'Natural Classroom', one where we are free to play, to find ourselves again.

If Nature beckons us, can we heed its call?

\#Play is memory

Des Vu

Day Voo

FRENCH

(Noun) the awareness that this too will become a memory

Play is enlightenment.

When we stand quietly with children among the trees, watch their toes touch the surface of a stream as they intrepidly paddle, or see children playfully encounter the world around them, then we glimpse childhood's intuition to explore and be curious – we see their joy-filled eyes that seem to glow as though temporarily mesmerised by the world.

It's as though play is the natural awakening to Nature's sensory invitation – it is the *becoming* of childhood.

With each breeze like Nature's breath on their skin; with every bare-foot step in the cool stream, the sunlight reflecting on the water as its surface ripples; with each choice children make and Play Pathway they follow, childhood is exploring what it may become – the moments of play transforming into a store of treasured memories as well creating and leading to the discovery of new propitious pathways.

What if we chose to seek the enlightenment of play too?

What paths might show themselves to us, and might these paths lead us to awaken to Nature's invitation too?

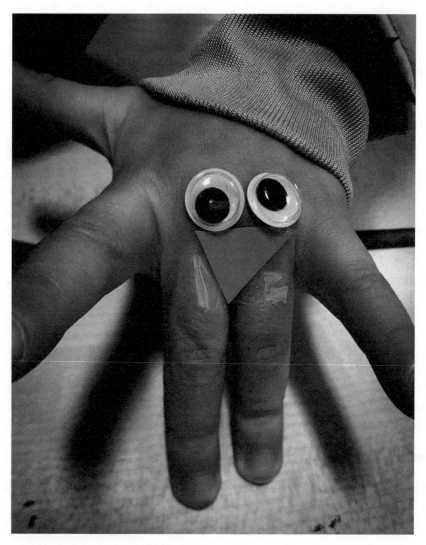

#Play is wisdom

Desbundar

Des-bun-dar

PORTUGUESE

(Verb) shedding one's inhibitions in having fun

Play is the 'wild' self.

Childhood lives in a world of unselfconsciousness, of an abandonment to delight, subversion and experimentalism, devoid of the social conventions and inhibitions that seem to entomb us in the Adult World. It's as though we slowly imprison ourselves within walls made of fear and self-doubt.

Childhood goes up the slide, we flounder at the very thought of it.

Risk is in the DNA of childhood.

It wants us to push past our perceived limitations, explore our own capabilities.

Where did our sense of Limited Life come from?

Who handed us this view of ourselves?

And, more importantly, are we really going to pass this on to children, who are showing us so brightly to let go of inhibition and enter the freedom of being?

Childhood wants to feel.

It wants to sense itself alive in the world, to dance and sing and create and dream, jump and skip and climb and build.

And if we were to take this moment to consider ourselves, to put down the heavy stone that the world has given us, then we might just see that we too want to do all those things and more in that constellation of possibilities waiting for us, not out of reach, but carried to us by childhood, the star bringer.

#Play is a force

Dormiveglia

Dor-me-veg-lee-ya

ITALIAN

(Noun) the space that stretches between sleeping and waking

Play is now.

Every day, a pocket of time. Every day, a pocket of possibilities.

Perhaps if we envisaged our time spent with children as mini spaces, ripe with the What Might Happen, then we might just glimpse how a child's life isn't term to term or stage to stage, but rather an ongoing series of waking hours in which we can adventure with them, each day containing its own treasure, its own unfolding.

Only when we look back, do we see how these days have led us to where we find ourselves in the present, for the road that childhood follows is paved within and by each day, writing its own map, its own journey.

When we close our eyes before sleep, can we say that the day we are saying goodbye to has been filled with adventure and dream? Can we fall asleep as the day lets go and know that we held childhood's hand within it and gave children time and space to be?

And when we wake is it with the urgent anticipation of all that lies ahead of us?

Of the possibilities waiting for us to find them, of the adventurer who knows that with each day that arrives there stretches something else: the kingdom of play and all its wonders.

#Play is being

Eleutheromania

El-oo-the-ro-mayn-ee-a

ENGLISH

(Noun) an intense or irresistible desire for freedom

Play is freedom.

When we offer play to children, we send them a subtle yet powerful message about the faith we have in them.

If we are open to liberation, to exploration and curiosity, then we show childhood that we trust it, that we believe in its creative spirit and its joy of wondering.

The impact of having faith in childhood cannot be overestimated.

When children play, they are themselves.

When they are denied play, they are forced to adopt a new role so that they can be accepted and feel like they belong – children begin to act outside their natural instincts, they have to 'unlearn' themselves, and they do this so that they can be praised and bonded with.

What if we gave children more freedom?

What might we see unfold before us?

Might we see people not personae?

Play is trying to show us a world of authenticity – perhaps it asks us to show our authenticity too …

#Play is marvel

Eshajori

E-sha-jori

JAPANESE

(Noun) 'people meet, always part'; the concept that expresses the impermanence of all things, that every human relationship will end someday due to the transient nature of life

Play is permanent.

Although time spent working with children might seem like snapshot-ism, we do in fact create a sense of self for them that lasts a lifetime.

Play sculpts the identity of childhood with every interaction, experience and moment.

We may feel that the bonds we make with young children are transitory, that they somehow outgrow us, but in reality, we are continually spinning a Golden Thread which entwines them with us and us with them.

This idea, that we are co-creating the self, is two-way.

As we shape children, they shape us – we become part of the same process.

In fact, it is as though we are processing one another. We take shape together.

Do the connections we make with children expire?

Play says no.

Instead, when play is with us, we carry bright shards of one another, like we have exchanged soul fragments, small glimmers of each other.

Perhaps that is what education is truly about?

The glimmering …

#Play is mystery

Eudaimonia

Yew-day-mon-ee-a

GREEK

(Noun) 'human flourishing'; a contented state of being happy and prosperous

Play enables.

Imagine play as an inner compass telling children what to do.

Can we feel that same instinct inside us when we hold expectations over childhood?

Are we above nature?

Can children be pulled from their instinctual selves and be equally enabled as they would be through play?

Perhaps we must first re-connect ourselves to our own innate sense of being – allow children to become our teachers; let them guide us.

Maybe if we are incapable of trusting in children, we are incapable of trusting in ourselves. Maybe play is an invitation to unlearn what we were taught, return to what we were 'de-Natured' from?

What does our own inner voice tell us about play?

Whether we 'decide' to play or deny it, what do our instincts tell us about why?

Is play attempting to enable us as it does children? Perhaps if we ask ourselves that question, we might begin to recognise that the trust we once had in ourselves can return.

Who might we become if we did that?

Imagine how the world might be if we had self-faith …

#Play is patience

Fernweh

Firn-vay

GERMAN

(Noun) a feeling of homesickness or longing for far-off places, even though you've never been there

Play is emotional.

Why do we feel so heartbroken when others dismiss play and replace it with control and Do This, Do That?

Is the root of our deep sadness the knowledge that childhood has a home, that it belongs in play?

When we offer play to children, we do so perhaps because we recognise it as the house we once lived in too.

Play begins to echo inside us, pulling us into the world of children's adventure and invention. It enriches us because we respond to children with memories of our past selves.

We see who we once were, we begin to recognise our long-forgotten capabilities – we become reunited with our selves.

We come back home.

We might ask why others don't feel the same heartbreak as we do.

What fear, what lack of self-knowledge, what mask prevents them from feeling as we do?

What do they sicken for? Profit, ego, power?

Where do these three lie within the possibilities of childhood?

Perhaps that is why they diminish play so readily – because it can't see their own self-interest.

Is that the home we want to live in? Does childhood?

Perhaps, our homesickness is a sign of our own redemption from the Adult World, a bittersweet pain, but one that shows who we truly are …

#Play is resilience

Fika

Fee-ka

SWEDISH

(Noun) a moment to slow down and appreciate the good things in life

Play is open.

What is it that we appreciate when we are in the company of children?

Where does gratitude live across each day spent with them?

Are we mindful of what play has shown us – not what we have taught children, not what we have seen them mimic, but what they have actually taught us?

Can children teach us anything?

How we answer that question reveals what lies within our soul. If we see that childhood can teach us, then we show something about ourselves – our open hearted-ness.

If we deny the lessons that children can show us, if we are solely fixated on task, readiness and the capitulation of childhood's dream, then this equally shows us who we are.

We are less a lesson to children, and more a lesson to ourselves. To learn this lesson, we have to find that space and time which enables us to look at who we are.

Are we a 'good thing in life' for children or are we merely functioning to prove our own worth?

The answer lies within us. Childhood holds up a mirror for us to see it …

#Play is the unimaginable

Fjaka

Fee-ya-kah

CROATIAN

(Noun) the 'sweetness of doing nothing'; a mood where mind and body drift in a total relaxed state

Play is daydream.

Drifting – when was the last time we did that in our adult lives?

When do we find ourselves adrift in thought and daydream, lost in timelessness?

When did we last feel the sweetness of being alive?

Isn't it this that childhood is trying to show us? Is it not revealing what life can be again?

The prevalent narrative of 'busy-ness equates to self-value' is rejected by play. It rejects it because all play is 'busy-ness', even that which involves loafing and taking time to wonder.

The self-value narrative creates a life that revolves around 'being seen to be busy', whereas play is a life that revolves around being authentically busy – busy doing nothing, doing, acting, being, thinking, hum and buzz or calm and quiet.

When we spend time in the company of children, we see that busy-ness is all around us, both outwardly and inwardly, and maybe, if we give ourselves permission to drift with them, children might teach us something about our own value – that it lies outside the narrative told to us, that there is a sweetness to finding ourselves busy doing nothing …

#Play is luminous

Fuubutsushi

Foo-but-soo-shee

JAPANESE

(Noun) the things, feelings, scents, images that evoke memories or anticipation of a particular season

Play is re-connection.

What joy do we bring to childhood when we adventure in the Natural World with it?

How do we show children our own affinity with it? Do we have one?

Through its seeming inability to imagine, the Adult World tries to remove children from its deep connections to the animal allies and the special places that exist all around them.

'Know the tree types' demands the Adult World.

Yet childhood is looking elsewhere - at the possibilities within the branches and roots. It wants to understand through heart-led immersion, through imagination, through wonder-full navigation.

'Know the parts of a plant' calls the Adult World while childhood looks in another direction, mixing potions and perfumes in the alchemy of the mud kitchen.

What if feeling came first?

What deep connections might we grow within children?

If the joy of the world was at the heart of it all? What then?

#Play is release

Galaxomas

Gal-ix-oh-mas

ENGLISH

(Noun) the passionate urge to live on a theoretical faraway planet that feels uniquely different to earth

Play is fantastical.

Stitched into the storylines of play, we discover that make-believe, that magical ability to dream up other worlds and other times, is a Golden Thread of childhood.

It is as though children have an innate ability to imagine the unimaginable, to conjure possibilities out of thin air.

Childhood seems capable of suspending reality at will, creating new worlds, where talking animals and adventure, extraordinary powers and Things Not Quite Making Sense are a matter of course.

Perhaps children have 'one foot in fantasy', and from there they bring an abundant richness of The Impossible into this world?

And their vehicle for this?

Play.

Do we enable children to show us their imagined worlds?

Or are we pre-occupied with our world of Do This, Do That?

What doorways that children show us do we pass through?

For the doorways to appear we need one thing – faith in childhood's dream.

Play asks us if we have it.

#Play is safety

Geborgenheit

Ge-bor-gen-heitt

GERMAN

(Noun) to feel completely safe, like nothing could ever harm you; security, comfort, trust, acceptance and love from others

Play is human.

Is the removal of play the annexing of childhood from its safety?

If play is a natural desire, then are we 'against nature' if we insist on standardisation, control and function?

Do we become less human in the moment we say no to play?

Play offers children a way to encounter the world and one another so that they might take risk, explore possibilities and slowly push themselves further outwards.

It does this by instilling in them deep emotional responses to their play-full inventions, role playing and collaborations.

Play brings childhood to life.

We might say that play offers childhood its spirituality, so if we are determined to evaporate it from children's days, then it speaks great volumes about our own …

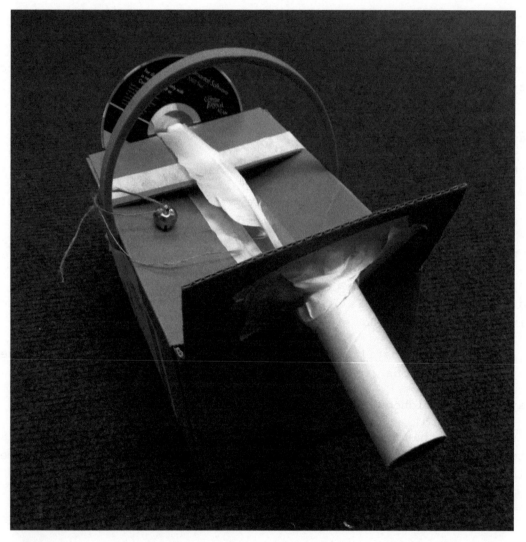

#Play is a retreat

Goya

Go-ya

URDU

(Noun) the moment when fantasy is so realistic that it temporarily becomes reality

Play is purpose.

When children immerse in play - really immerse in it - it's as though the 'real world' dissolves and another one comes fading into view.

The storylines, the being, the make-believe, the 'Things Becoming Other Than Their Intended Purpose', all of them revealing a New Reality, a landscape that boils with dream, the cascade of possibility.

And all this opens the door to a question whose knock we faintly hear throughout our lives, a question that reaches our ears when we sense there is another world inside this one, a question that asks:

'Whose world is this?'

To whom does this world belong and how do we shift away from its constraints so that we might move wholeheartedly into the realm of who we truly are?

And childhood reveals the answer, the answer that we know deep within us: that there is a world we glimpse in the corner of our eye, that we half-know, half-remember.

It's a world that lives in the simplicity of play and The Warm Hand of Simple Things.

It's time to go there, again and again and again …

#Play is transformation

Gunnen

Gun-nen

OLD DUTCH

(Verb) to find happiness in someone else's happiness because that's how much you love them; to think someone deserves something

Play is time.

What do children deserve and, more importantly, when do they deserve it?

We talk endlessly about 'life chances' and 'future earnings', all the while setting sights on some distant unknown point in time rather than the one childhood exists in.

So here we come over the hill with flag unfurled, 'More, Earlier', to a chorus of loud trumpets, all the while trampling over the Dream of Now that childhood lives and breathes in.

What if we gave children time?

What if the flag that bears the words 'More, Earlier' blew in the breeze of giving children more childhood, more space, more of themselves?

Could we possibly envisage a world where children were immersed in the joy of living for longer so that the academia could be found by them and not foisted upon them in some great Phonics Tsunami, some great tidal wave of 'This Is The Only Right Way'?

Play asks us if we are able to discover our happiness in children's happiness, in their joy and choice, in their discovery and freedom.

It waits for us to answer …

#Play is unlearning

Hiwaga

He-wa-ga

TAGALOG

(Noun) mystery; full of wonder

Play is inquisitive.

What are we curious to know about children and play?

Perhaps play is less of an answer and more of a question mark held up against the world.

It's as though each day contains a magnet pulling on childhood's heart with all its strength, drawing it onwards to explore and unearth. The strength of this magnetism depends greatly on whether we create the conditions for it to show its force.

It's in the learning landscape we prepare, the play we enable and the rhythm of the day. It's in our co-playing, in our voice and our own bodies, it's in all the things we share and add to childhood's dream.

And for children to be full of wonder, for them to sense it running through themselves, responding to the magnetic pull of the day's mysteries, we need to find our own, we need to become 'wonder-full' so that children see our own sense of curiosity, not only about the world, but about them - who they are, what ignites them, what immerses them in the adventure and how.

It is our curiosity that in turn enables that of childhood - when we give children room to 'ask the question of play', it is then that we adventure too, the curious adult hand in hand with the curious child …

#Play is a response

Hozho Naasha

Ho-zo Naa-sha

NAVAJO

(Noun) to 'walk in beauty'; to walk in harmony with all living things; the state of awareness where you find beauty and feel connected to everything around you

Play is wandering.

When we wander, do we have a clear route, do we have a determination to only arrive at a set destination come what may? Play reminds us of the opposite – that wandering, our adventure in the day, allows us to see the enchantment and wonder of the world, to notice.

Perhaps this is one of play's greatest reminders – that to live is to see, to allow the day to show itself. Only when we allow ourselves to wander, do we connect to all that is around us.

What is it that we are trying to connect children to?

What emotional response to being alive in a world that teems and boils with sensory delight and possibility do we show them?

Do we walk in beauty with children?

What if we enabled childhood to wander – what might the world show them and, in turn, what might childhood show us?

#Play is action

Hyompora

Hi-om-por-a

ENGLISH

(Noun) the sense of serene connectedness experienced while listening to the flowing of water

Play is remembering.

What if we focused on the idea of 'connection'?

Teaching to connect, not teaching to prove, enabling play to root children in themselves and the world, rather than the perpetual Can They Do This-ness we offer them?

How might play truly glow throughout each day if we saw childhood through this lens?

Are we capable of being more connected to our own days too, to return to the creative adults we know we have hidden deep inside us?

And here, it is play that reveals itself since it is the 'Prime Connector'.

The Adult World may come running over the hill, but what is it connected to?

What has it forgotten or been made to forget?

And what prevents it from a re-connection to what it has lost along the way?

#Play is metamorphosis

Iksuaropok

Ik-su-ah-ro-pok

INUIT

(Noun) the feeling of anticipation when you're waiting for someone to turn up

Play is time together.

It holds the same emotions as those moments when you wake up and *that* day has arrived.

That excitement which seems too much to bear – continuous checking of the time, looking out of the window. Time seems to stand still – the hands on the clock aren't moving! Are they here yet!?

You catch sight of them, run to the door. They are finally here! But it isn't just about the arrival of the person and their presence – it is the essence of what they bring as they cross the threshold and join their world with yours.

The world of togetherness, the euphoria of re-connection, of reminiscing, memories shared and made, each new moment the beginning of a future memory to hold in heart and soul.

It is this same energising power that exists in play.

'Shall we go for that walk, you know the one where we built that den in the woods? What about when we were hiding between the corn crops? That huge spider! Or that time we filled our wellies with the river water and ran back and forth up the hill, back home, to see if we could fill buckets with it? Or that time we slipped and fell down the hill, into those stinging nettles!!! Do you remember that dance we created? Shall we go and play …?'

Play is connection and belonging – it is love.

And if play is love, do we belong to it?

If we don't give play to children, then what do we belong to?

#Play is security

Ipseity

Ip-say-it-ee

ENGLISH

(Noun) the quality of being oneself

Play is visionary.

Play shows us that the routes to growth do not necessarily lie along the same path for every single child.

Yet if we look around it seems as though the individuality and uniqueness of childhood have slowly, *tragically*, been eroded.

We have a world where conformity subtly but consistently frowns upon, shames and punishes the unique mind.

The free thinking of play doesn't fit the mould, doesn't balance with the standardised set-in-stone statue travelling along the conveyer belt of our systems.

If from birth, childhood is saturated with the need to 'learn against itself', we sink it beneath the wave of standardisation.

Where are the free-thinking children?

Where are the healers and inventors of the future possible world, those who can change and evolve hearts, communities, the world?

Are we able to say that we have shaped generations of them?

Through imagination, creativity and risk, play shows us that these children can live and breathe, that we *can* believe in a better future ...

For those children are there playing in the puddles, the mud and grass, in amongst the trees and piles of sticks, the painting easel, the blocks and the playdough.

They are before our very eyes learning and navigating the world, but only if we enable play.

Through running, spinning, jumping, rolling, climbing, building, exploring and inventing children are building the new future.

Play asks us: 'What would a future look like if you let children play?' – it demands an answer, it demands our own free thinking ...

#Play is risk

Isolophilia

I-so-lo-phi-li-a

ENGLISH

(Noun) strong affection for solitude, being left alone

Play is capability.

Do children need to be with adults to learn?

What happens when we let go, what adventure could be sparked into life and how might children feel if they were given greater autonomy within their days?

The more we compress childhood around curricula and 'What You Have To Learn Because I Have To Get You To Learn It', the more we diminish children's abilities to be self-reliant and to dig deep within their own natural resources of being born a learner.

And the more we do that, the more the Adult World concocts ways to prod children into trying to learn what they have little interest in learning about.

Where does this lack of children's interest come from?

The answer sits so clearly before us: from the erosion of play with all its natural growth mindset and inclination and wonder and intrigue.

What if we let children be for longer?

Might we then discover that they do care to learn - that they're just waiting to be left alone in the world of their fascination and song to get on?

#Play is dream

Kadan

Ka-dan

SANSKRIT

(Noun) 'where the heart lies'; an all-purpose word for a person one cares about, including friends, family and loved ones

Play is me.

Imagine if play wasn't a 'thing', but a person.

In fact, imagine if it was more than a just a person, but the best friend of childhood, someone who children confide in, whose company makes them feel alive, who they want to be with every waking hour.

Perhaps if we were able to personify play in this way it could help us understand why children are so connected to it and its possibilities.

Could it help us see why it is so important for children to hold the hand of play?

That each moment we separate them from her, we cause them to leave where their hearts belong?

Do we hold the hand of play too?

If we deny children play – with all its choice, creativity and curiosity – we are culpable of breaking a powerful mental and physical bond. We become 'separatists'.

Yet conversely, if we offer play's hand to childhood, we become 'forgers of friendship', we strengthen the bond that, in a way, children *have with who they are*, because they are childhood, as though they hold hands with themselves …

#Play is pattern

Kairos

Ky-ross

GREEK

(Noun) the perfect, delicate, crucial moment; the fleeting rightness of time and place that create the opportune atmosphere for action, words, or movement

Play is legacy.

One childhood, once. It's not repeatable.

We can't go back – there's no return ticket.

As adults we seem to spend vast amounts of time trying to heal from our early life, attempting to recover from the lessons that were etched within us: lessons about who we are, our place amongst others and our place 'within ourselves'.

When we enter the world of children with all its burning curiosity and wonder, it's imperative that we see its fragility, that every day we recognise how we hold this delicate world in our hands, hands that must gently guide not lead, reassure not control, protect not admonish.

The days of childhood may seem fleeting, but their legacy lasts a life-time.

How do we give children the legacy of self?

There's a treasure to be unearthed in the days of play – a treasure of the Creative Self and of the Curious Mind. It can be found in every action, every word, every movement.

To discover it, we first have to see the 'rightness' of play and then it will show itself, burning like a million suns …

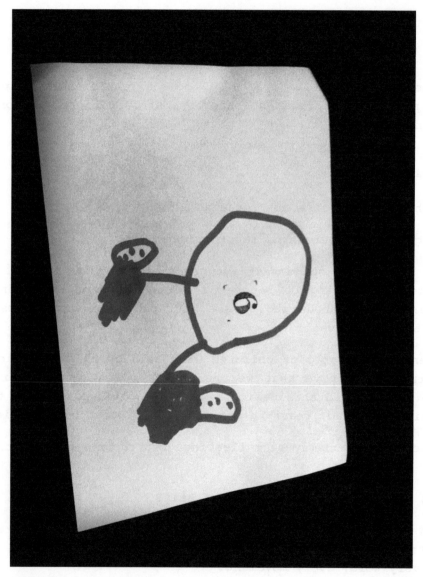

#Play is urge

Kawaakari

Ka-waa-ka-ree

JAPANESE

(Noun) the glow of the river or stream in darkness or dusk, the gleaming surface of a shadowed river

Play is light.

Perhaps play's greatest 'weakness' is that it somehow lies beyond the reach of precise language – it can't be easily substantiated or weighed, it can't necessarily be made transparent for us to dissemble and contain within the cells of Spreadsheet Living.

It's as though play is a mirage, a glowing light that shimmeringly shows itself, but, at the very moment we try to touch it, evaporates before its very eyes.

This is the elusive nature of play – something that, although powerful and essential in the truest meaning of the word, slips through our fingers the moment we attempt to grip it.

Perhaps we should try less to understand play and more to simply feel it.

Can we feel play?

Maybe that way we could break out of our own entombment, maybe then we could see how play insists on feeling before function, just like all life should do no matter what age – the glow, not the darkness …

#Play is wild

Kilig

Ki-lig

TAGALOG

(Noun) the feeling of butterflies in your stomach that you typically feel when something romantic happens

Play is a romance with the world.

How do children feel about coming into our setting each day?

What do they sense will be awaiting them?

Do we create the conditions for childhood's heart to sing with anticipation as it makes its way towards us?

If we believe that childhood wants exploration, invention and dream, if we truly believe in the possibilities of play, then 'adventure' has to be at the centre of our narrative.

Can we adventure without choice or in 'days-as-task'?

When should childhood's adventure end, and who ends it?

#Play is capable

Koi No Yokan

Koy No Yo-kan

Japanese

(Noun) the feeling of excitement when you first meet someone and know that you will eventually fall in love

Play is love.

What if love made a comeback in the story of childhood?

And if the gift of play is an expression of love, could play lead us back to learning with joy and adventure?

Has the Adult World made 'love' a forbidden word, so that it can keep us from who we truly are, from our instinct?

Do we step into the world of childhood without love?

If we enable play then certainly not, since play gives children freedom. It is letting go, love's greatest act.

We may not agree that telling children we love them is 'right', but we must accept that we can at the very least show children our love by who we are in their company as we adventure together.

If we give childhood the gift of play, then we give love.

We will feel it inside us.

We may not say the word, but we can sense it.

It will be in the room with us.

#Play is motivation

Liberosis

Lib-er-oh-sis

ENGLISH

(Noun) the desire to care less about things – to loosen your grip on your life, to stop glancing behind you every few steps, rather, always in play

Play is fortitude.

What holds us?

Money? The pursuit of acceptance? Possessions?

How children in their play are trying to teach us!

We recognise that play is a force within childhood, but we perhaps see it less as one that works on us too.

In the world we inhabit that seems so intent on brittle living, play reminds us of our possibility for change and growth, it's creativity and wonderment whispering to us to remember ourselves.

Play shows us the glimmers of our potential to be softer, more open, more invested in who we are – it shows redemption …

#Play is life

Livsnjutare

Livs-n-ju-tare

SWEDISH

(Noun) an enjoyer of life; one who loves life deeply and lives it to the extreme

Play is illumination.

Does childhood exist at the edges of life?

It's at these boundaries where children find the nourishment for mind and muscle, where risk can be found, gleaming and exhorting children to climb and jump and hunt and test. This is play in action - children going beyond their self-perceived limitations, all the time not only exploring the boundaries of life but pushing them out further and further, creating more room for themselves to adventure in.

And it is here that we can come to a grinding halt because we no longer live at the luminous edge of All Things Possible.

Instead, we are chained to The Known and What Has Been Forgotten, trying to exert a force on childhood to bring it away from the edges of life and towards our limited store of learning that sits bereft in the darkness and rust of forgetfulness and fear.

So, we have two equally strong forces pulling on children's very core: the exuberant adventure of childhood and the cold grip of Do This, Do That.

One offers the infinite, the other offers limitation.

One pulls on children because its force is open-heartedly yearned for, the other pulls on children because it is afraid to leave its sanctuary.

Childhood wants to exist at the edges of life - perhaps we need to join it there.

Who knows what we might find?

#Play is story

Luchtkasteel

Lu-kast-eel

DUTCH

(Noun) 'air castle'; a wish or dream one hopes to fulfil in the future, yet will never be achieved as it is so vast, immense and unlikely

Play is dream.

No dreams, no change.

Can we imagine education taking on a different form, one that goes way beyond what is accepted, what is given?

Play can.

Play dreams of a life that values and honours childhood, that immerses it within authentic creativity and curiosity.

It dreams of possibility, of re-imagination, of 'Things Can Be Different'.

Play invites us to see that what seems unachievable can be transformed into The Possible.

It just asks us to dream and dream harder …

How are we dreaming, or have we stopped?

If we have stopped, then why? Did we choose to, or has something outside us ended the dream?

What will we do if we know?

#Play is musicality

Madrugada

Ma-dru-ga-da

PORTUGUESE

(Noun) the moment at dawn when the night greets the day

Play is a hello to the world.

If we greeted childhood, how might life look?

Would play not show its capacity to shake the day from its stupor, would it not energise each moment with its delight and discovery?

And how might we greet play? With reserve or with open welcoming arms? Would we hug it and hold it tight, cherishing all that childhood has to offer us?

However, what if it was the other way round? If we allowed childhood to greet us instead?

Does play not wait for us to find it?

Does play not open its arms each day so that we can be embraced by all its wonder and marvel?

Do the days belong to us to unlock, or is it childhood that holds the key?

Just what is it that we say hello to each and every day?

#Play is encounter

Mai-tri

My-tree

SANSKRIT

(Noun) the art of developing unconditional friendliness for oneself

Play is sacred.

Might we describe play as 'childhood being in harmony with itself'?

Or perhaps play is the steps towards this harmony as though it lies in some future self, waiting to be unearthed, each play-full act bringing it closer and closer to fruition.

If so, then this might just be the adventure of play itself – the quest into self-connection, into the creative spirit.

Do we deny the adventure of play?

If we deny it, if we curtail play and all its possibilities, then we sever the cord that childhood has to its Sacred Self.

We become agents of alienation.

If we as educators are also denied play, both for ourselves and our children, then we too are being self-separated.

Which is why play never has been the sole domain of children. It is who we are – it is our harmony too.

#Play is the unknown

Manawa

Ma-na-wa

HUNA (NEW AGE)

(Noun) 'now is the moment of power'; to be not bound by any experience of the past, nor by perception of the future; having the power in the present and constantly planting the seeds for a future of your engineering

Play is now.

We can often get caught in the narrative of 'the future' and 'readiness' and, when we do, we lose sight of the childhood that stands before us – we overlook the adventure of the day at hand and instead find ourselves living in fear of the future, we become enveloped in a story that does not belong to childhood.

Can we live in the present moment?

Children do.

It is their reminder to us and what play is showing us: that only when we are present are we able to see and feel the enchantment of the day's adventure.

Play tells us that the future will be shaped in this day, not tomorrow. The explorations and inventions, the discoveries and the connections with the Right Now will enable children's 'readiness'.

It's as though play is revealing the need to let go of the future and asking, if we are surrounded by voices that demand we don't, what is being revealed about them?

#Play is wonder

Meliorism

Mel-ee-or-ism

ENGLISH

(Noun) the belief that the world gets better; the belief that humans can improve the world

Play is progress.

How can the world get better? And what can it get better at?

The answer to both questions is buried somewhere in the potential adventure that childhood can be.

If we enable children to choose, create, collaborate and dream, if we value those dreams and open our minds and hearts to learn from them, then we have a greater chance to shape a world we might want to see.

To do that requires us to take on a Great Task - to unlearn ourselves, to see that children need to have a place in their own days, to recognise that play and its freedoms are what the world can be.

Wherever play lives, lives the future too. To deny play is to deny The Future That Could Be.

Do we have the courage to confront ourselves, the parts of us that cling to what has always been?

Play improves the world - when children play they reveal its multiple possibilities.

#Play is speculation

Merak

Meh-rak

SERBIAN

(Noun) a feeling of bliss and the sense of oneness with the universe that comes from the simplest pleasures; the pursuit of small, daily pleasures that all add up to a great sense of happiness and fulfilment

Play is elating.

What gives us Soul Float?

What makes us feel the elation of being alive?

The answer to those questions more often than not is rooted in the Things That Are Freely Given To Us By The World – family, woodland, the company of animals, the sea, birdsong, quiet time pottering in a garden or the warm hand of someone you love beyond all others.

And yet somehow these things can be paled for us by the 'pursuit' of possession, property and the 'Disneyland-ification' of life that tells us to feel we must go somewhere and pay for the privilege.

Do the birds bill us for their song? Does the sea that sends its murmur deep into our soul invoice for its joy? Does the dog at our feet request payment before it flaps its ears with that 'hud-hud-hud' that somehow reaches into us and lifts our spirit for one joyous moment?

It is to this sense of 'personal proximity' with the World that we need to return – something that childhood asks us to do too, since day after day after day it invites us to open our hearts to play and its pursuit of those small, daily pleasures of building and drawing, inventing, exploring and of being who you are meant to be.

In fact, we might say that childhood is sending us a message in everything it does:

'Inhale the World. Breathe it deep and breathe it long …'

#Play is a map

Meraki

Mer-ak-ee

GREEK

(Noun) to do something with soul, creativity or love; the act of leaving a piece of your self in what you are doing

Play is energy.

When immersed in the flow of play, childhood grows outwardly - it is led to the optimum of consciousness.

It seems like play leads children to a place where there is no longer a sense of time, but rather of wonder and experimentation where discovery and understanding can be found - children discovering Discovery.

It's as though play creates new realities, opens doors into Waiting Worlds, each one offering a powerful burst of living, of being.

What energy do we allow for children?

What if play *is* the energy that education needs …?

Is childhood asking us to add to its energy, not diminish it?

If we allow play, what gates will it open and what new energies might come pouring into the world in which we live?

Perhaps play demands our energy, it requires something from us.

But can we give it?

#Play is allegiance

Micawber

Mi-caw-ber

ENGLISH

(Noun) an eternal optimist; one who lives in optimistic expectation of a better future

Play is the future.

What do we mean by 'a better future'?

What does it look like and what does the Adult World mean by it?

Is it possible to forge one if children are removed from play and given days of Do This, Do That? Does it not undermine the possibility of that very future in the act of rote and test?

The Adult World speaks so much about democracy and individualism, of choice and innovation, yet congeals the days of childhood into standardisation, targets, performance and output. It talks of 'life chances' whilst eroding the very creativity and inventive drive that runs through children's bloodstreams. It disconnects them from who they really are - what a life it gives them …

What if we gave children an education that truly served them?

What if we raised them, not 'taught at' them?

What if interest and allowing children to flow into learning and vice versa was our vision?

Is that really so unimaginable?

And what if parents were a-livened to the possibility that they should expect a Better Present, one that revered who their children really are?

What then?

#Play is solidarity

Mudita

Moo-dit-ooh

SANSKRIT

(Noun) taking delight in the happiness of others, vicarious joy

Play is elation.

Play ripples with joy.

Whether it be the intense feeling of delight after children have taken risks and seen that they are capable of facing their own limitations, or the rapture of running, of chasing, of the sense of being free to move and explore, play sparks a response that resonates deeply in childhood.

Contentment, wonder, thrill - all are part of play's pursuit.

What joy do we unlock for childhood in the days we spend with it?

We will know if play is alive because we will feel its joy pulsing all around us and inside us, for play opens up the possibility of happiness at the happiness of others.

In a way, play makes us 'self-less'. It enables us to let go of ego and instead draws us into solidarity, a community encountering the richness of the world and one another.

We take delight in play and we return it too, joy giving birth to more joy, just as childhood wants life to be.

#Play is destination

Mukaya

Mu-ka-ya

JAPANESE

(Noun) 'non-existence'; the natural state as it is, finding meaning and purpose in emptiness; to see potential in a void; 'an empty room will be filled with light because of its emptiness'

Play is weightless.

Does every last minute of childhood need to be plotted and filled with the Known?

What if our plans no longer insisted on a long-term fixed trajectory that takes children in a direction they never really asked to go in?

What might we witness?

If we made space for choice and creativity, for play to show itself within the learning landscapes we provide for children, then childhood could bring us its remarkable gift for transforming emptiness, for 'making something out of nothing'.

Perhaps this is play's purpose? To show us the joy of empty spaces and how to use them as catalysts for adventure, invention and dream.

How we over-structure children's days, how we compartmentalise and narrow time!

But childhood says 'No'.

It wants emptiness and what it will fill it with can be greater than any adult mind could possibly imagine …

#Play is architecture

Murr-ma

Mer-ma

WAGIMAN (AUS)

(Verb) to walk along in the water searching for something with your feet

Play is seeking.

Where do children's feet take them and when and why do we prevent them from going there?

Is childhood the time and space for adventure, exploration and discovery?

To unleash children's footsteps upon the world – perhaps that is what play is telling us to do.

For wherever the feet go the heart follows …

The searching feet of childhood lead it on the Journey of Wander Wonder, as though each step is trodden in curiosity and trial.

Perhaps this is the real test that childhood confronts – the test of self, of surety and confidence, a test not led by hands alone but by feet too.

And perhaps it's not the feet that lead the heart, but the heart that leads the feet …

#Play is a doorway

Nakama

Na-ka-ma

JAPANESE

(Noun) friends like family

Play is bond.

It is powerful attachment and energy between children and one that can include the adults who have the privilege to be in their company. Its strength lies in its authenticity, its realism.

When children play, it's as though they become even more open to one another, more 'socially supple'.

There is an unspoken-ism within play that quietly pulls children in and holds them in its spell together.

Childhood seems to accept The Code, the morality that amplifies as children's games and explorations emerge and involve.

It's as though children have an affinity with one another even before they've met, a recognition that play is a family that they already belong to.

What glimpses of The Code do we witness each day? And are we accepting of it and accepted by it?

Are we part of the family of play?

#Play is magnetic

Nam Jai

Nam-Jay

THAI

(Noun) 'water from the heart'; genuine acts of kindness without expectation or strings attached

Play is mental health.

We would certainly have a strong case to argue that the increase in mental health difficulties over the years and the prevalence of behavioural problems in childhood are the results of play deprivation, of the replacement of choice with control.

What might children's view of themselves be like if we invested more time and space in play, if we truly valued it so that its richness could become the principal predictor of the future?

What possibilities might lie ahead of us if we brought self-love into the narrative of success?

What change might play bring into the world?

Perhaps the difficulties we see are manifestations of childhood's spirit begging for the hydration of play - could play be the reminder of what we need to value once more - love, kindness, creativity, collaboration, a genuine unconditional care for the world in which we live?

If our current systems are built to serve The Economy, where is the water for the soul, for the heart of who we are?

Where are the refreshing waters of play?

#Play is rhythm

Natsukashii

Nat-su-ka-shee

JAPANESE

(Adjective) joyously reflecting on fond memories, not with a wistful longing for the past, but with an appreciation of the good times

Play is capable.

How do we know who we are?

How are we defined by the memories that transform inside us and give birth to the almost supernatural inner voice that either pushes us onwards or naggingly holds us back from our own possibilities?

What future memories lie ahead? How are we to meet these and sense ourselves making them?

Play is the Memory Maker of childhood.

Each moment that we afford children play is a moment in which powerful, irrevocable memories are being forged. And here, memory is less about rote and knowledge base and more about that voice inside us, that commentator on capabilities that seems to tell us who we are and what we can do and be.

Play - the catalyst of Self.

When we deny play, we deny the Self. When we welcome play, we embrace the Self.

What memories are we making for children?

What will they remember about themselves and how might we make the days of childhood ones that burst and bloom with memory after memory after memory …?

#Play is an unfolding

Nefelibata

Ne-fe-li-ba-ta

SPANISH

(Noun) one who lives in the clouds of their imagination; an unconventional person

Play is unique.

Perhaps play's greatest power is its ability to show children's unconventional-ism.

Or maybe play *is* 'conventional' but is slowly denied and replaced.

When we look at childhood, what storylines do we see pouring out of it, what tropes make themselves known to us?

Do we see the common plots of architecture, design, exploration and invention? And what are they telling us?

If play is an act of research, perhaps it's not of children but of ourselves.

Could it be that it is not the story of children that we observe when they play, but of us?

Is play trying to show us something about our own self-narrative?

Does life have to be written for us or, maybe, if we recognise what we are being shown by the gleam of play's bright ray, are we able to write our own story – one that illuminates who we truly are …?

#Play is energy

Nepenthe

Nuh-pen-thee

ANCIENT GREEK

(Noun) something that makes you forget grief or suffering

Play is 'forgetfulness'.

When children immerse in play, it seems to allow them to let go of the world and slip into a state where trouble is forgotten, even just temporarily.

It's as though play absorbs childhood, offering a realm of remedy.

Is play then some kind of trance-like state, offering an illusory sense of detachment from life?

Is there a possibility that children are actually conscious of this effect, that they somehow *know* play, they understand what lies within it so they seek it?

Do adults carry this consciousness too?

Is that what frightens us about play?

Do we fear the act of letting go, of losing the sense of control?

Have we forgotten that within the landscape of play there lies the possibility of healing?

Perhaps play is trying to help us remember to forget …

#Play is potential

Noroke

Noh-rok-ee

JAPANESE

(Noun) the way one constantly speaks with fondness and enthusiasm about one's love

Play is the Mother Tongue of childhood.

Is it a language we have to learn or one that we must re-learn?

Perhaps play is children's way of communicating The Extraordinary Of Life, speaking not only about themselves but about us too.

If we believe so, then play can sweep over us and in us, filling our own minds once more with the possibility of possibilities, with marvel and with an eagerness to notice the joy of simple things - play, the living language.

What does every block tower built, every line drawn, every role acted out by children tell us?

What does play spark within us?

If play doesn't ignite us, then how do we speak in a world that was intended for play?

What language do we attempt to shout over its golden voice instead - is our voice one we believe in, or is it one with which we, without heart, lamely echo the dead words of the past without spirit, without joy?

#Play is alchemy

Novaturient

No-va-tur-e-ent

LATIN

(Adjective) desiring or seeking powerful change in your life, behaviour or a certain situation, soul searching; the feeling that pushes you to travel or take up a new hobby, experience new things and break free from your current reality

Play is valuable.

We're not robots.

Neither are we function nor 'factory set'.

Play shows us possibilities – that children and teachers CAN be creative, they CAN bring themselves into their days and, above all, they CAN break free from what would try to entomb them.

And we can do this when we begin to search our souls for who we are.

The more soul we search, the more soul we find – the more soul we find, the more soul we show. Every moment of showing our soul to children brings the day when play and childhood are truly valued closer and closer.

Are we robots?

Or are we flesh and blood with hearts that beat with the joy of Being Me?

It is who we are that childhood is looking for after all, not a Template Teacher …

#Play is captivating

Numinous

Nu-min-ous

ENGLISH

(Noun) *feeling both fearful and awed by what is before you*

Play is amazement.

What if we opened ourselves up to be marvelled by play?

What might happen to us if we looked beyond What Is Demanded and glimpsed The Joy of Childhood Unfolding?

Would it move us away from the fear that is so readily instilled within us?

Each day when children play they are showing us something that we can be astounded by. When was the last time we felt astonished at what lies before us?

Can a worksheet or template bring us into a world of awe and wonderment?

Every day we deny the possibility of play we equally deny the possibility of ourselves – we negate our capacity to be awestruck, we become 'week-ended and holidayed', contracting our own and childhood's potential of spending each and every day in The Remarkable.

#Play is a spell

Nunchi

Noon-chee

KOREAN

(Noun) the subtle art and ability to listen and read the room; literally 'eye force/power'

Play is faith.

What if play was asking us to trust in childhood as something sacred, something connected to its intuitions, to its True Self?

If we acknowledge that play is in part a deep need to feel connected, something that begins from birth with a baby's desire for touch and proximity to the skin of a caregiver, then we can see how play has such a critical role in feeding childhood's instinct for survival, for nourishment, for growth.

Childhood has a pure voice of Nature speaking inside it, a voice it needs to tune into to navigate danger and grow. Yet we seem to have created a world that has increased the cacophony of expectation on children that drowns out that voice, forcing it to call out louder:

'Do not leave me; do not disconnect; do not place me in a box of expectation.'

It is as though what has become normal has become adversarial - we confine childhood by removing children *from themselves*.

Perhaps play is a manifestation of that inner voice's plea?

'Keep me close, allow me to be, nurture me as we learn and play together.'

Maybe childhood knows what is happening to it?

What if instead we optimised childhood by looking to be more like our hunter-gather ancestors; validating children's needs, being with children as the naturally co-operative and worthy learners they truly are?

What if we listened to childhood?

#Play is sacred

Osusowake

O-soo-so-wak-ee

JAPANESE

(Noun) sharing with others what has been given to you

Play is a gift.

Play is continually trying to give us possibilities: learning, strength, wonder and words. It wants to give us the senses so that we can glimpse The Remarkable.

Play knows our shortcomings and our fears, and it had within it the courage and tenacity to confront and overcome them in the adventure of our own childhoods.

Play gives children what they need most.

What is our gift to childhood?

Are we determined to remove the gift of play for children so that we can give them ours?

How are the days of childhood spent with us - in submission or in awe?

If we give children compliance and conformity, then this is the result of our own shortcomings that play once knew and could have guided us past. If so, we have forgotten play or had it forgotten for us; we are left with a meek submission of our own - we give the 'gift' of instruction and task in days emptied of possibility.

The moment we fail play, we fail childhood - and the moment we fail childhood, we fail ourselves …

#Play is magical

Oubaitori

Oh-bai-to-ree

JAPANESE

(Noun) the idea that people, like flowers, bloom in their own time and in their individual ways

Play is gift.

Perhaps childhood has a clock – its wonder, creativity and exploration deeply rooted in time itself, as though each day is marking the natural movement forward, 'keeping time' at its own pace, tentatively but accurately, the hands being exactly where they should be – time within its own time.

To speed up that clock, to try to turn its hands by force, begins to wear the fragile mechanisms that enable the clock to tell the right time in the first place. And what keeps those hands ticking? Play!

If we deny play, we are, in some way, denying time.

We are trying to accelerate children beyond themselves.

Could we give childhood more time?

Might we see it bloom as it should?

Imagine what life could become if play, with all its richness and possibility, was given more scope!

Could the gift of two more years of play, with its abundant richness, show children the joy of mathematics and words but without the meddling of the hour hand, so that the clock of childhood might tick tock as it can and should?

What then? What might we see?

Is it really a sign of having low expectations to wait for learning to flow with children or is that simply a myth of the Adult World to continue haunting childhood with the spectres of the past?

#Play is remarkable

Philomath

Phil-oh-math

ENGLISH

(Noun) a lover of learning

Play is becoming.

Whatever we learn to do, when we 'play at it', we *become*.

The world around us was born out of play, out of its invention, its ingenuity, its curiosity.

What great power play truly has!

Our most famous inventors of the world invented thorough play – electricity, light, sound, vehicles, travel, materials, food and on and on and on, all products of play's Great Adventure.

Through play – the *freedom* of exploration and of failure – we have been led to discovery and invention.

Play made the world become.

Yet has play somehow 'become less', has it been forced to exist in isolation, as something we grow out of?

What if we let play *become* once more?

What might happen to the world if we saw play as the powerful, prevailing creator that is it?

And who might we become?

#Play is identity

Piliriqatigiinniq

Pil-iri-kwat-ig-een-ik

INUIT

(Noun) togetherness; community spirit, working together for the common good

Play is a force.

When children come together in solidarity, when they collaborate and 'join forces', we glimpse A Life That Could Be. We see the reality of Possible Futures.

The co-operative soul that lives within children – that drive to work together to see what can be made to happen, what can be built or found or shaped – still echoes in us as adults.

Play reminds us of how we once lived before we were alienated from one another by individuation, economy and class.

Which force do we value most?

In the depths of children's collaborations we see the echoes of how life can be – alongside one another, protagonists together, journeying and moving forward, sharing and wondering side by side.

And, yes, children can also play alone and be apart from one another in their own dream, but these times are all part of the community of childhood that shows children acceptance and the joy of being together or not together – we separate to come back as one.

We are part of something beyond our immediate selves, even as adults, all of us connected by the one thing we share in common, the one thing that IS the common good: play.

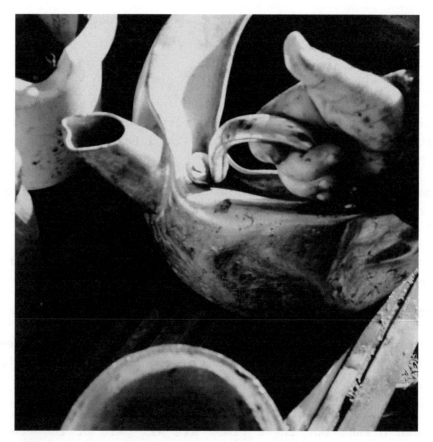

#Play is invention

Pronoia

Pro-noi-a

ENGLISH

(Noun) the belief that the universe is conspiring to support you; the opposite of paranoia

Play is communion.

There is a universe that blooms with heartfelt story and song, that amplifies the unspoken yet powerful bond with the Beyond Human world. This universe is play and it gives childhood its greatest possibility, that of adventure.

Play offers a wondrous voyage with the companionship of animals and one another, the busy-ness of the hedgerow, the company of trees and the wind, and the guardianship of the sun and moon.

It is a Universe Of The Wild Heart and it calls to us.

Children hear its voice and respond, echoing back with its play-fullness, its inventions and its dreams.

Perhaps this is what play truly is? Childhood responding to the universe with its silent roar …

Can we hear the Universe Of The Wild Heart?

And if so, what if we responded too?

#Play is wonder

Psithurism

Sith-yer-iz-im

ENGLISH

(Noun) the sound of wind in the trees and the rustling of leaves

Play is sound-ful.

What is it we bring to childhood's adventure?

What gifts do we carry with us to share with children as they go about their day?

If play is what connects children to the world they find themselves in, then what we bring with us must strengthen those connections not diminish them.

Perhaps the joy of spending time with children is less about 'teaching' them and more about 'highlighting to' them, showing them that which is hidden but can be found.

In amongst these highlights, we can share the soundtrack of the world through our noticing and attention. Birdsong, the wind, the singing stream, branches creaking, planes overhead, the traffic in the street, all combining to the Surrounding Song.

And this joy can be amplified further when we highlight how play joins in this song too; the snipping of scissors, the thud of feet, the clack of wooden blocks, the plop of paint.

All this, and every moment of play, part of the Great Soundtrack of Nature, of childhood, of living …

#Play is solidarity

Qarrtsiluni

Kwart-sil-un-ee

Inuit

(Noun) to sit quietly together in the dark

Play is invitation.

Play can be movement, play can be stillness. It can be energised or contemplative.

However it shows itself, play is an invitation – both to other children and to us.

Play invites children to join in and it invites us to learn from it.

When we take time to watch play unfold, as we sit quietly alongside childhood and see what possibilities emerge, we begin to see that all of life is here: enquiry, experimentation, connection, exploration and dream.

It may seem simple, but play is doing great work within children – it is telling them who they are.

In our days with children, how much of them sees us sitting quietly, taking in the unfolding adventures?

Play has a great adventure to take us on even when we are still …

#Play is affinity

Rasasvada

Rus-aas-vaad

SANSKRIT

(Noun) the taste of bliss in the absence of thoughts

Play is a message.

Are we capable of change?

Can we look inwardly upon ourselves and see the need for greater imagination, for more soul, more dream?

Perhaps play is childhood's urge to dream.

And in this dream, children enter a state akin to 'unthinking thought' – an absorption into the world around them, unconscious of the internal and physical developments that are occurring for them as they play. It is as though they are thinking while not thinking, being while not being.

We might say that play is instinct – the urge to let go and become temporarily 'lost'.

Maybe this is what play is looking for – our own ability to change.

Where can it be found?

#Play is rarified

Retrouvaille

Ruh-troov-eye

FRENCH

(Noun) literally 'rediscovery'; a reunion (e.g. with a loved ones after a long time apart)

Play is you.

Who were you before the World told you who to be?

Do you miss them?

Do you look back and sense the creativity, the vitality and the wonder that somehow got left behind in the past of childhood years, that you were separated from?

Can you ever go back and meet that child again, embrace them and invite them into life once more?

Perhaps play is like a magnet to our memories, pulling on us as children play.

Perhaps it is a force from our own past; less what we see before our eyes in the Right Now and more a series of glimpses sent from our own childhoods, travelling through time to speak to us, to remind us of who we truly are.

Can we reunite with our five-year-old selves?

Is it possible? Play says a resounding 'Yes'.

To hear its call, we only need to become 'open sensed' – for when we do, we'll hear play echoing from all those years ago. 'Take your five-year-old's hand,' it says. 'It's been a long time apart but that five-year-old will lead you because it knows where it's going – right back to who you really are, back to your bright ray, your possibilities, your self …'

#Play is spirit

Riyaaz

R-yaaz

URDU

(Noun) to practise a form of art every day

Play is potential.

What is the art of childhood if it isn't play?

Can we envisage how remarkable children's play might be if we allowed them time and space to rehearse it by immersing them in opportunities to dream and bring themselves into their days?

If we were to embrace play, we could create the potential for children to 'get better at it'. If we gave childhood the adventure that it truly deserves, then imagine how powerfully competent they would become at adventuring.

What might the play of a seven-year-old look like if they had been equipped with the tools to continue their 'art', if each day had furnished them with opportunity on opportunity to submerge in exploration, wonder and invention?

Perhaps we could see the abundant potential if we practised an art too – the art of imagining …

#Play is home

Ruhe

Roo-ha

German

(Noun) peace and quiet, when nothing around you bothers you and you feel calm and good; also the designated quiet time in a neighbourhood

Play is dimensional.

Play can be expansive and boisterous, full of vitality, hum and buzz. Yet it can just as equally be calm and silent, more withdrawn and shell-like.

It doesn't need to prove itself to our perceptions of 'How Life Should Be' that seem to compress and constrict all that childhood might possibly be.

How do we acknowledge and respect the many faces of play?

How do we enable childhood to find its way?

And how does our Time Together embrace the varying energies that contract and expand across each day?

When we begin to consider the Rhythm of the Day rather than the worn-out narratives of timetable, adult-led, carpet time etc. we can begin to put ourselves into the day with children.

We can take the conscious steps into how the day 'plays out', into the adventure, something that the Adult World finds almost impossible to do in its mire of How Things Have Always Been.

The Rhythm of the Day offers liberation, not just in our movement but in who we are, because who we are holds within it as much kaleidoscopic energy as childhood does …

#Play is soul

Ruska

Rus-ka

FINNISH

(Noun) the phenomenon of leaves turning various shades of red, yellow, purple and brown during autumn

Play is pathway.

In fact, we might say that play is multiple paths, since it offers a universe of possibilities to children - some well-trodden, others formed by surprise and the shock of the new.

Perhaps this is why we should enable play to live at the heart of childhood - so that, by immersing ourselves in innovation and invention, we might learn new ways of seeing and being, we might learn how to change.

Play is showing us one clear path that we need to tread first, one that eventually leads to all the other pathways that wait for us when we have faith in childhood, one that leads to the discovery of who we are.

But if we are reluctant to seek play's pathways, where are we leading children instead, and what joy, comparable with the ones paved by play, will be found there?

#Play is search

Sampajanna

Sam-pa-jan-nah

SANSKRIT

(Noun) clear knowing, full knowing

Play is a force.

Play allows childhood to take hold of life.

It is an instinct - a pursuit of liberation and self-governance.

Yet play's ability to do this, to shape learning and develop the courage to navigate life, can only happen if we allow it.

By enabling play, we give children a deep connection to us and shape a world around them that is built on an encompassing, non-conditional trust in their abilities.

Where there is play, there is faith.

Does childhood need reward to follow its natural drive and innate desire to hear, listen, watch and learn?

Does it require carrots for its curiosity and marvel, or sanctions/praise to earn acceptance, to be loved?

Play allows children to 'be'; it *is* value.

For when we enable play, we are giving permission to childhood to follow its own natural, intrinsic motivations, and it is within these that we discover children's authentic sense of growth and achievement.

Play is not a reward to be given, but a reward in and of itself.

#Play is liberation

Sankofa

Sang-koh-fa

AKAN TWI

(Noun) 'to go back and get it'; represents the importance of reclaiming our past so we can move forward; going back to our roots to understand why and how we became who we are today; the wisdom of using past experiences to build the future

Play is truth.

What possibilities might spring to life if only we could somehow shake ourselves from the malaise of ego and profit before people?

What rich childhoods might we forge if we were capable of opening its eyes to what shackles it in the past?

Where is the vision beyond The Economy?

Where is the Imagined Life?

Have we really become so depleted in our understanding of who we are and how we got there?

How can we return to who we used to be before individualism and 'possession-as-self-worth' took hold?

If only there was a way that we could lead it by its hand and return.

'What are you afraid of?' asks childhood as it plays.

What will we answer? Truthfully?

#Play is potent

Satnam

Sat-nam

GURMUKHI

(Noun) 'I am truth', or 'Truth is my essence'; an expression of your true identity, not only for the benefit of yourself but also for others; you are connected to all there is - the vast universal truth

Play is veracity.

In spite of all the voices that try to dim its light, play and the urge to play can never be completely taken from children. It is who they are.

This is the Permanent Truth. It's as though childhood is loudly declaring: 'I AM PLAY.'

And how do we respond? Do we echo back the same?

Are we play?

Do we feel it coursing through us and out of us even though the world would have a different, more diminishing narrative for the story of our lives?

If we are play, we are truth.

If we offer play to childhood, we send it a powerful message about how we see our own essence.

Perhaps this is the question that play demands we answer:

'Are you true to yourself or is something else speaking for you?'

#Play is vigour

Seatherny

See-thern-ee

ENGLISH

(*Noun*) *the serenity one feels when listening to the chirping of birds*

Play is a song.

Life needs a soundtrack, and arguably the time of childhood needs one the most.

Outdoor play isn't solely about physicality and exploration.

It has an even deeper, critical role to play – to immerse children in the subtle, yet infinitely rich musicality of the world around them.

If we believe that children belong outside, then what is out there that they belong to?

Is it not also the birdsong, the wind playing within the trees, the far-off drone of traffic, the ebb and flow of a soundscape that lies beyond the door?

When we pull children's attention to the Sounds Around, we open their ears to the music of the world, so that when they're climbing and running, building and jumping, they too join the song with their laughter, thud of feet and whoop of heart.

Childhood has its own notes to add to the world's orchestra which is waiting outside.

We just need to open the door so they can reach it and join in.

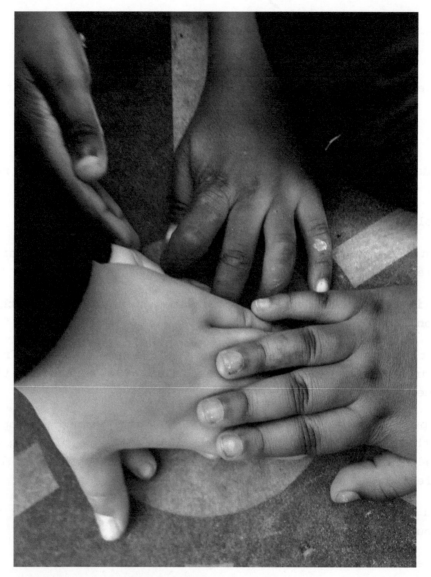

#Play is dependable

Shinki-itten

Shin-ki-it-ten

JAPANESE

(Phrase) a fresh start, turning over a new leaf, to change one's mind, a new beginning

Play is renewal.

When children play, they bring newness to the world. They refresh it with their wonder and invention. It's as though childhood sculpts with life - moulding it into meaning.

In each moment of sculpture, play renews.

With every creation, every possibility, play shows itself as an act of imagination and marvel that transforms and liberates.

And as it does so, play calls to us as well, beckoning us to the edge of who we think we are, asking us to open ourselves to the possibility of our own renascence.

Play wants us to change because it knows our capabilities, even though we might have buried them beneath the layers of persona that we so expertly make for ourselves in our own childhood experiences.

Are we able to begin again?

Play offers us a pathway to rejuvenation. It offers us revivification.

If we can hear how play calls to us, if we are willing and know that, deep within us, we can find faith in play once more, then our adventure of rebirth can truly begin …

#Play is bond

Shoganai

Shyo-ga-nai

JAPANESE

(Noun) something that cannot be helped, being unable to alter or change a situation; take it or leave it

Play is Natural.

What might we change so that all children can have an abundant childhood?

Can we delve into our imagination and picture just how different life could be for our youngest children?

Have we the capacity to see how play, with its all its rapture and wonder, could transform their experiences, could bring us as adults into the days of delighting in the world too?

Are we so heavily laden with the weight of 'How Things Have Always Been'?

Can we dream differently and begin the adventure into transformation?

Play shows us that the world can be re-imagined. See how childhood takes the worlds of ideas and objects and language and sense in its hands and reshapes them?

There lies our own lesson – it's what play has been trying to remind us of: change is possible when we act.

#Play is fascination

Shoshin

Sho-shan

JAPANESE

(Noun) a Buddhist term meaning 'beginner's mind'; an attitude of openness and eagerness for whatever you encounter in life; a willingness to set aside preconceptions and expectations

Play is the beginner's mind.

We might say that play is 'blank'. Yet this blankness must have something to be connected to, and this is why childhood seeks play - to attach to something.

It's as though when children play, they begin to be.

We might benefit from putting down our own preconceptions of what life is and seeking to adopt the mind of the beginner.

Perhaps childhood in Indigenous communities that rarely show the discontentment of 'civilised society' has something to show us?

Does the 'continuous attachment' of the in-arms phase with all its safety and connection - children sleeping, feeding and living immersed in the rhythms that surround them - create a more harmonious community?

Through exploration and curiosity, ingenuity and the unrushed handing down of wisdom, indeed through play, do their children learn what they need to become part of their world, of their future?

Do we recognise the trust here in Nature - the instinctual understanding that children can find their way?

Perhaps this is what play is showing us about so-called advanced societies - that we need to be more empty-minded, be increasingly open to looking beyond ego and conditioning.

For when we do, we might glimpse the universal truth of play: that it is life itself.

Maybe then we might try to learn play's lesson …

#Play is plot

Sib ncaim

Sib-chi-um

HMONG

(Verb) to part ways after a brief encounter, never to meet again

Play is encounter.

Can we feel our own play-fullness humming and buzzing inside us?

Can we sense the store of joy that has its home deep within us, the one that reminds us of the adventure that can be unlocked within every day we spend in the companionship of childhood?

If we can, then it is this that we have been separated from; we have been dis-located from our natural joy and wonder, from our creative soul that brims with story, song and play, and re-homed in the cold, damp house of formula, function and Do This, Do That.

In doing so, we are not only diminishing play, we are diminishing ourselves.

The systems of control that entomb us don't want us to return to who we are; they need to restrict us to being who they want us to be - a deliverer of scheme and programme, an object in the chain of micro-management and accountability. They want us to forget the person we once were.

But there is one thing that acts as a constant reminder of this person, like a faded photograph on a shelf, a picture that may be bled of colour, may be curled at the edges, but is still there calling to you.

And that one thing is play.

It tells us that we are not a formula.

We don't have to part ways with who we are - we never should have been made to leave them and now it's time to make that encounter with our true selves - not brief, but last a lifetime.

Rise up and play. The time is now for us to write Love Letters to Play every single day before it is too late …

#Play is passion

Sillage

Sill-idj

ENGLISH

(Noun) the scent that lingers in air, the trail left in water, the impression made in space after something or someone has been and gone; the trace of someone's perfume

Play is 'trade'.

Perhaps play is like a transaction, a way of leaving impressions on one another. In fact, it might be better to say, leaving impressions **in** one another, since this is what play does - it shapes the soul.

When we play, we exchange: language, action, idea, skill, role, warmth and possibilities.

When we see play in this way we begin to sense its extraordinariness, its deep connectivity.

Play is no longer solely the domain of the visible; it is the invisible too, forming something inside each of us through every invention, exploration and discovery.

Through play, we learn about and from one another. Play is asking this question over and over:

'Are we willing to learn from children?'

We share ourselves, which, it could be argued, is the greatest transaction we can ever make …

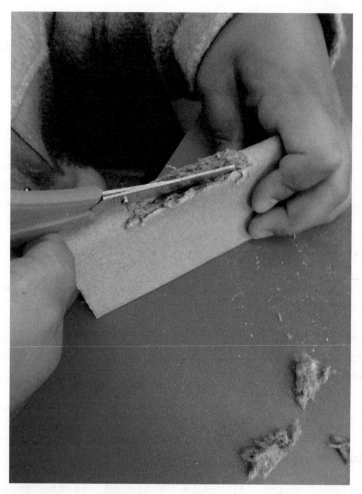

#Play is vision

Sobremesa

So-bre-me-sa

SPANISH

(Noun) the time after lunch or dinner spent talking to people you shared the meal with, the people you love

Play is proximity.

When we think about the days ahead that we will spend with children do we ponder the adventure that we will share with them?

Are we going to pull childhood into our pre-mapped plan or are we open to enabling the days be an unfolding, allowing children the possibility that anything is possible?

Play is telling us that the soul is here for its own joy - childhood wants to play and it invites us to come and sit at its table.

There is a space waiting for us. The invitation is there because play loves us - it hasn't forgotten us.

Play has always been at our side waiting for our return.

Do we want to play?

What great and powerful things might happen if we chose to requite play's love for us?

#Play is innovation

Sodaba

So-da-ba

PERSIAN

(Noun) someone who is unique, visionary and different from others; literally means 'pure water'

Play is ingenious.

The visionary-ism of children can be astounding if we allow it to be.

Time and again, if we enable children to be protagonists in their days, if we give them choice and show them that their autonomy is valued and wanted, children are perfectly capable of shocking us with their hum and buzz of invention, imagination and making the impossible seem possible.

Each day that children enter our learning spaces, they do so full to the brim with wonder, with the urge to show themselves for who they are - a desire to dream, to question, to create coursing through their veins.

If we are able to unlock ourselves from the 'What Has Always Been', if we can break out from the entombment of the Adult World, then the visions of childhood are shown for what they truly are - wave upon wave of potent reminders to remember our own visions, our own half-remembered dreams.

For it is in these dreams, however dusty or cobwebbed, that our true selves live.

'What are the visions you once had?' asks childhood.

Whatever we might answer, childhood says in a loud voice: 'Dream them once more and live again!'

#Play is rich

Soham

So-ham

HINDI

(Verb) I am he/she/that; to identify oneself with the universe or ultimate reality

Play is the World-As-It-Could-Be.

We seem to have shaped a world that has disconnected us from the most basic, raw needs of the people we might be, who we naturally are.

Play, however, shows us the possibility of a different world within its macrocosm, one far removed from the tick boxes that seem to have pulled us so far away from what we so desperately require, from how to live authentically, how to *thrive*.

That World-As-It-Could-Be still exists within us - we are reminded of it by every child because it lives in play.

What if we were brave enough to free childhood and lead it back to the possibility of deep discovery, back to the natural wisdom that has been within children from the day they were born?

What if we reclaimed childhood?

What Natural Nourishment could we see unfold before us? What world might we create for ourselves too?

#Play is ingenuity

Sonder

Sohn-durr

ENGLISH

(Noun) the realisation that every passer-by has a life as vivid and complex as your own

Play is complicatedly simple.

In a world that seemingly wants linearity and step-to-step-to-step, play stands to one side. It has a paradoxical simplicity that is, equally, complex.

It's as though play won't fully reveal itself so that we have to go in pursuit of it, we have to earn the right to fully understand it.

Perhaps because play is ever-evolving it creates new ways of being and seeing that tangle us with complexity - we think we know play, but then it goes and surprises us once more. It's as though play can't be fully contained, offering us small pieces of itself then, in the very moment we think we have understood, it transforms them to reveal something.

And this might be because play is so tied to emotion. It gives play a transience that lies beyond collection and confinement, as though to know play we have to come with Feeling Not Function. It demands our full curiosity.

Are we curious about play?

Do we want to know it completely?

Perhaps this is the adventure that play offers us?

A lifetime of exploration and wonder - not only of childhood, but our own inner landscape …

#Play is inspiration

Sturmfrei

Sturm-fry

German

(Adjective) the freedom of not being watched by an adult or superior; being alone at a place and having the ability to do what you want

Play is autonomy.

Do children always need our company to learn?

Can children be trusted?

Do we have faith in their ability to immerse in the world around them without us being at their sides?

Are they capable of collaborating and chatting and lifting one another up without us?

What freedom we offer children if we answer 'Yes and here is play!' and what rich possibilities we open up when we show them our faith in their autonomy and choices, what message they receive about themselves when we let go of the need to control every last inch of their days!

If we are to shape days based around what childhood so richly deserves – exploration, creation, joy and discovery – then children's ability to lead their own way must be at the heart of them.

And as we ourselves become more like companion guides within those very days of wonder, though we may be taller and older, and wiser perhaps, we know that to let go is adventure itself.

For there can be no quest ahead of children if compliance and control dominate the day – it's why we as adults hold the key – not to unlocking childhood, but to unlocking our very selves.

Because it's not just childhood's freedom that control separates us from – it's our own …

#Play is cathartic

Sukha

Su-kha

SANSKRIT

(Noun) genuine lasting happiness independent of circumstances

Play is joy.

Is play the home of happiness?

What feelings burst inside children as they play, and are these replicable through any other experience?

What is it that play holds so uniquely in its palm that makes childhood sing so loudly with its joy?

Perhaps the answer lies in the synchronous enrichment that springs to life when children play.

Through play, children embellish the world by applying their forces of invention and curiosity to it – they mould it to their will, they take objects beyond their intended purpose, *they liberate them.*

And in return, objects in the hands of playing children offer back an equal enrichment, inviting them to enter a world-as-playground, a place that welcomes re-imagination, that wants to be transformed.

The world of objects holds its breath waiting for us to play with it, in the same way that childhood does at the thought of freedom, choice and encountering it.

Children need to play, and objects need to be played with – it is a lesser world without.

#Play is healing

Tarab

Tuh-rub

ARABIC

(Noun) being enchanted by music; the way music makes you feel; the trance experienced by a strong connection to music

Play is immersion.

When children play, they sink into life as though it was velvet.

By shaping landscapes for childhood to adventure in we create the conditions for enchantment, for children to be held by spells that spill out and surround them.

And it is this enchantment that can absorb us if we are willing enough to be drawn in, if we set aside The What Has To Be and instead embrace The What Can Be.

When we find ourselves inside the dream of childhood we discover the spell that lives inside of us too.

How do we spin the world together with children and what magic do we see pouring out?

Perhaps we might even say that we are in the greatest need of childhood's dream.

When was the last time we felt the velvet of the world?

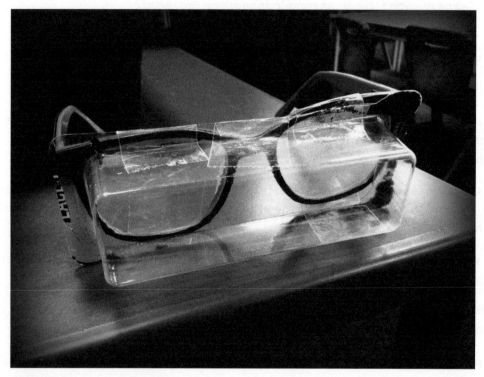

#Play is insight

Tri hita karana

Tree Hit-a Ka-ra-na

BALINESE

(Noun) 'three causes of being'; harmony among people, Nature and the universal energy

Play is being.

What kind of force is play?

Is it something that separates us or joins us together?

Is it individuation or solidarity?

Perhaps if we saw play as a 'cause of being' we might come to a richer understanding of its universality, of its 'common language' – the joy of feeling alive among others and the Natural World.

When we look at play in the light of the three causes of being we see life in accordance with what it can be, we glimpse our affinity with the Beyond Human world and each other.

Perhaps if we observed children and looked less for 'developmental tick-listing' and more for 'connection' we might shift the narrative around play towards a way to being, a universal and essential energy – an expression of our very humanity.

Do we see the three causes in our days with childhood?

Do we sing their song?

Might we sing it louder, and what if we sang it to parents?

What universal energy might play bring into the world?

What then?

#Play is research

Turangawaewae

To-ron-ga-way-way

MAORI - NEW ZEALAND

(*Noun*) *'a place to stand'; a place where we feel rooted, empowered and connected; this is our foundation, our place in the world, our home*

Play is home.

What if we saw play as childhood's home?

What if we thought about the peace children find within the four walls of play?

Maybe then we might wonder how childhood so invent-fully and skilfully furnishes this home for itself; might we also consider more carefully how long it wants to live there?

Perhaps if we pictured play as childhood's rightful home we would have less inclination to break our way into it with Do This, Do That?

What if we began to envisage how we can be invited in, how we could bring gifts with us - tools to make more furniture perhaps? By doing so how might we be transformed from 'housebreakers' to house warmers …?

#Play is daydream

Ukiyo

U-key-oh

JAPANESE

(Noun) literally 'the floating world' – living in the moment, detached from the bothers of life

Play is birth.

Who brings the bothers of life to children?

And why?

If childhood truly is the world that floats above us, then perhaps it should stay there. Instead of bringing it down to Earth, should we instead try to join it?

To float upwards, so we too might detach from the bothers of life, we will need to discover what makes that children float – dreams and curiosities, adventure and exploration: we might even say that their world is held up by the very 'spirituality' of childhood.

And it is this spirituality that childhood requires us to find within ourselves too – to take our own adventure, one that leads inwardly, that demands us to seek the examined life of who we are and why we are, to discover our own spirit, our own soul.

It asks us to see into ourselves, to look our motivations in the face and to choose whether we want to float upwards or cling to the ropes which we attempt to pull on to drag that floating world crashing down to our ashen Earth.

Only once we have taken that adventure can we truly say we are ready to be in the company of children.

Only then will childhood help us live again – because that is what it can do, waiting in its floating world.

#Play is loafing

Unalome

Oo-na-low-m

SANSKRIT

(Noun) a symbol for the journey to enlightenment; it reminds us that the path isn't always straight, perfect, or even in the 'right' direction; our path to awakening is filled with missteps, lessons to learn and suffering

Play is landscape.

If we believe that childhood is worthy of a glorious adventure, if we have faith in play and the choices of children, if we shape days in which they can 'find themselves', then we equally create the conditions for them to get lost along the way.

We must also accept that this is part of the journey itself – that failure and frustration are just as valuable as the moments of success.

Play knows that learning is not linear and observable, that step doesn't always follow step in a neat row. Play has a myriad of paths that can be followed.

What map is there that might show us the ways childhood wants to follow? Why, it is drawn by play itself!

How do we create a landscape where we truly explore and navigate with children?

Are we willing to look up from the well-trodden path and explore instead the pathways of childhood?

Down those, we might discover more than just the joys of invention and adventure – we might also, just like the children, find ourselves …

#Play is craft

Wabi Sabi

Wa-bee Sa-bee

JAPANESE

(Phrase) *loving someone for who they are; the acceptance of transience or imperfection*

Play is success.

Play shows children that to be successful, they must fail along the way. It tells them that success isn't immediate and doesn't have to be - that our imperfections make us perfect. We move forward through failure.

And since play is an adventure that requires us to 'get lost' now and again, curiosity - with its vast universe of questions and intrigue - has to be at the heart of the time and space of childhood.

So, play asks us:

'How do you make childhood an adventure, and do you allow it to fail so it might learn its own strength, its own heart?'

'How do you enable children to follow the pathways that shine at them as they explore?'

When we offer play to children we are accepting them for all of who they are - we show them our loyalty - we are welcoming childhood to live alongside us in the kinship of failure and the discoveries and understanding that it might lead us to.

#Play is pioneering

Wu Wei

Wo Way

CHINESE

(Noun) effortless action; actions that do not involve struggle and excessive effort; the mental state in which our actions are effortlessly in alignment with the flow of life

Play is flow.

Childhood wants to float along on its Stream of Play-fullness.

It is on the stream and at the same time it IS the stream, its currents created by the forces of invention, adventure and marvel.

When this stream is in full flow, we see the remarkable possibilities of childhood, and when we value play, we too can step into the stream and allow childhood to float us on and on.

Perhaps it is the fear of stepping from the certainty of The Known that so inhibits us from ever discovering where the stream leads.

Maybe this is what play is asking us:

Are we brave enough to take that step in to childhood's flow and, if so, are we open to being carried along with it?

If we are prevented from taking the step, then what is preventing it? Whatever it is, it is not only inhibiting play, it is also inhibiting us …

#Play is you and I

Xibipiio

He-be-pee-oh

PIRAHA

(Noun) experiential liminality - 'to go in or out of the boundaries of experience'; the act of just entering or leaving perception - that is, a being on the boundaries of experience

Play is portal.

Play is a liminal world - a doorway that appears and beckons us to step through, to leave our 'reality' and enter another.

In this way, play can be seen as an invitation to surrender, to let go of our own 'surety' and pass into the unknown of childhood's dream.

To take this step, there will be internal struggle, uncertainty and fear because we don't fully understand or know what lies on the other side of the doorway in the unmapped landscape of play that stretches out before us.

Where do our portals lead?

The liminality of play draws us out of The Known and into a transitional space, one that questions our senses of order and structure, and of control.

In a way, whenever we have enabled play, we have confronted and embraced our own vulnerabilities, our own 'self', since we must do that for play to spring to life.

And it is through this confrontation that play can bring change within us, as though play has some kind of 'chrysalitic' power over us - it offers us the possibility of inward transformation.

So, when we see play in this way, we might also see that it is a gift - not one that we give to children, but one they give to us.

Part Two

Other Love Letters to Play

Other Love Letters to Play

You may want to consider the joy of the following words, allow them to sink in and then think about how they might be a catalyst for your own reflections on play and childhood …

Ailyak

(Ail-yak)

BULGARIAN

(Noun) the subtle art of doing everything calmly whilst enjoying what you're doing and your life in general

Arbejdsglæde

Ah-bites-gleh-the

DUTCH

(Noun) 'job joy' or 'happiness at work'; the heightened sense of satisfaction you get from having a great job

Besa

(Be-sa)

ALBANIAN

(Verb) 'to keep the promise', honouring your word; to make an oath; to keep faith in one's word

Chantage en yaourt

Ya-ort

FRENCH

(Noun) hearing a song and needing to sing along even though you don't know the lyrics, using nonsensical noises that vaguely resemble the actual words

Dépaysement

De-pays-mon

FRENCH

(Noun) the feeling of restlessness that comes with being away from your country of origin; feeling like a foreigner; literally means 'to be un-countried'

La douleur exquise

La do-lur ex-queez

FRENCH

(Noun) 'the exquisite pain', the pain of unrequited love

Fachidiot

Fak-id-iot

GERMAN

(Noun) 'subject-idiot'; a person with expert knowledge in their own field but who has no idea when it comes to anything outside of it

Guanxi

Gwan-shee

CHINESE

(Noun) connections or networks; a strong personal relationship with someone involving moral obligations and the exchange of favours

Hinna

Hin-na

SWEDISH

(Verb) 'to be on time' or 'to find the time'

Ikigai

E-key-ga-ee

JAPANESE

(Noun) 'your life purpose' or 'a reason for being'; to have a purpose in life which makes it worthwhile and full of meaning; also a small, daily ritual you enjoy

Jijivisha

Gg-vee-shaa

HINDI

(Noun) the intense desire to live life to the fullest; a person who lives intensely and seeks to thrive

Kaamos

Ka-moss

FINNISH

(Noun) the need for sunshine; a feeling of depression from darkness and bad weather, no social life and little inspiration

Mít kliku

Mit kli-koo

CZECH

(Verb) to have luck on your side; literally means 'to have a door handle'

Mokita

Mo-kit-a

KIVILA – PAPUA NEW GUINEA

(Noun) a commonly known truth that no one wants to admit or talk about

Nepakartojama

Ne-pa-kar-to-ya-ma

LITHUANIAN

(Noun) a once in a lifetime perfect situation; literally, 'unable to repeat'

Ré nao

Ray nee-ow

CHINESE

(Adjective) 'lively' or 'bustling': a fun place that makes you want to be there

Schlimmbesserung

Shlim-bess-er-ung

GERMAN

(Noun) something that was meant to be an improvement but in reality made things worse

Taarradhin

(Tah-ra-deen)

ARABIC

(Noun) the act of coming to a compromise that suits everyone; a reconciliation that all are happy with

Uitwaaien

Oat-vye-en

DUTCH

(Verb) to go out in windy weather to refresh and clear one's mind

Voorpret

Voor-pret

DUTCH

(Noun) the build-up of anticipation and joy ahead of an actual event; literally means 'pre-fun'

Part Three

The Green & Black books

"EVERY MOMENT IS A FRESH BEGINNING"

T.S. ELIOT

IN THE ACT OF PLAY, CHILDREN REVEAL
THEIR 'WHO-NESS', LIKE A BUD IN THE
BRIGHT SUNSHINE OF A SUMMER'S DAY,
THEY OPEN THEMSELVES, UNFOLD + SHOW
US THE PSYCHE + ITS WONDER...

PLAY CREATES TRANSPARENCY:
THROUGH PLAY, WE SEE CHILDREN
FOR WHO THEY TRULY ARE...

LIFE ISN'T EMPTY - ITS RICHNESS
STANDS BEFORE US + WAITS WITH
ARMS WIDE OPEN READY TO WELCOME.
AND PLAY IS THE SAME, ITS VAST
WEALTH STANDS BEFORE US - TAKE
THOSE FIRST STEPS + NEVER LOOK
BACK...

THE ADULT WORLD LIVES IN A STATE
OF FEAR, OF WHAT-IFS + STOP-DREAMING.
IT EXISTS IN AN ANXIOUS HOUSE,
AFRAID OF OTHERNESS + POSSIBILITY.
YET CHILDREN ARE SENDING US A
MESSAGE: PUT DOWN YOUR FEAR, RELEASE
THE GRIP OF MIS-PERCEPTION + EMBRACE
THE WONDERS OF THE WORLD - THERE
AREN'T SEVEN, THERE ARE INFINITE.

RE-IMAGINING A WORLD WE FORGOT
TO REMEMBER...

PLAY IS THE ULTIMATE BOX OF DELIGHTS.
TRANSFORMATIVE, EMPOWERING + CAPABLE
OF TRANSPORTING US OUT OF TIME
+ INTO THE REALM OF POSSIBILITY

WE NEED TO LOOK TO FIND IT...

CAN PLAY SAVE THE WORLD? WHAT IF PLAY ALREADY IS THE WORLD? IT'S JUST THAT WE'RE BLIND TO IT OR WE'VE TRIED TO REPLACE IT? PERHAPS CHILDREN REVEAL THE TRUE WORLD TO US – FREEDOM, SOLIDARITY + EXPLORATION...?

IS CHILDHOOD WHERE WE LIVE OUR TRUE SELVES?

IS CHILDHOOD THE ONE TIME IN WHICH WE ARE CONNECTED TO OURSELVES, ONE ANOTHER + THE WORLD?

THE CONNECTIVITY OF PLAY

INVITATION + ACCEPTANCE

PLAY 'SEES' ALL

PLAY MOVES US FROM 'PRE-CONCEPTION' TO 'RE-CONCEPTION' - IT OFFERS US THE OPPORTUNITY FOR ADJUSTMENT FROM THE TYPECAST TO THE LIQUIDITY OF ACTION, THOUGHT + SELF-PERCEPTION.

PLAY IS MOVEMENT - OF THE BODY + OF THE SELF : IT IS 'ANTI-STATIC'

THE UNKNOWN + UN-KNOWINGNESS

WE CANNOT FORESEE PLAY, WE CANNOT SECOND-GUESS IT. THERE IS NO 'FUTURE', ONLY THE NOWNESS OF THE EXACT MOMENT.

WE SINK INTO PLAY, WE DON'T DAM THE FLOW BUT WITH FAITH STEP INTO IT + ALLOW OURSELVES TO BE SWEPT BY ITS CURRENT.

YOU CANNOT 'KNOW' PLAY. YOU CAN
ONLY 'UN-KNOW' IT. BY 'UN-KNOWING'
PLAY, WE UN-KNOW OURSELVES WE
RELINQUISH THE ROLE OF POWER-HOLDING.
WE SUBMIT TO THE WILL + ENERGY OF
CHILDREN.

WE RE-DEFINE 'KNOWLEDGE' - IT IS NOT
WHAT WE KNOW, BUT WHAT WE CAN COME
TO KNOW.

WE PURSUE THE UNKNOWN

WE BECOME DEFINED BY WHAT
WE DON'T KNOW.
WE ARE, WHAT WE ARE NOT.

UNDERSTANDING IS SHAPED BY
WHAT WE DO NOT UNDERSTAND YET

THE MYSTERY OF CHILDREN

THE EDUCATOR IS DEFINED BY WHAT HE OR SHE DOES NOT KNOW, BY WHAT HAS NOT YET BEEN REVEALED TO THEM.

THE EDUCATOR BECOMES CONSCIOUS OF THEIR 'NOT-NESS'

THE OPEN DIALOGUE OF DISCOVERY

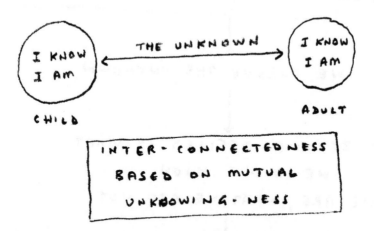

I KNOW I AM

THE UNKNOWN

I KNOW I AM

CHILD

ADULT

INTER-CONNECTEDNESS BASED ON MUTUAL UNKNOWING-NESS

WHEN WE LET GO OF CONTROL, WE LET GO OF THE PAST + ENTER AN AUTHENTIC EXCHANGE OF DISCOVERY + UNFOLDINGNESS : THE REVELATION OF IDENTITY...

PLAY IS LIKE A DANCE, A DANCE THAT NEEDS TO BE LEARNED + RE-LEARNED WITH EACH NEW MOMENT. IT IS A DANCE OF ANYTHING-NESS — ITS STEPS CAN TAKE CHILDREN IN ANY DIRECTION. IT IS NOT PREDETERMINED, RATHER IT IS IN A STATE OF PERMANENT EVOLUTION...

THE DIRECTIONLESS-NESS OF PLAY

PLAY IS AIMLESS-NESS : IT IS A DRIFT OR LIKE THE WIND IN THE WILLOWS

IT IS LIKE TRYING TO CONTAIN WATER IN A SIEVE — PLAY ESCAPES 'INTENTION'

PLAY HAS A MIND OF ITS OWN...

IT THINKS IN THE LANGUAGE OF THE INFINITE

* ANYWHERE-NESS *

WHEN WE ENTER CHILDREN'S PLAY, WE SHOULD TREAD CAREFULLY WITH SOFT FEET + TENTATIVE STEPS.

IF WE RUSH IN, WE LOSE THE POSSIBILITY OF ADVENTURE, WE 'LOSE SIGHT' ONLY SEEING THROUGH THE EYES OF EGO.

WE BECOME PLAY-BLIND...

WE NEED TO ENTER THE WEAVE OF PLAY WITH SENSITIVITY + HUMILITY

PLAY HAS A UNIQUE FRAGILITY. A DELICATE UNSEEN SPELL THAT IS EASILY BROKEN + THEN LOST.

WHEN WE INTERACT WE NEED TO ENTER A STATE OF PLAY CONSCIOUSNESS...

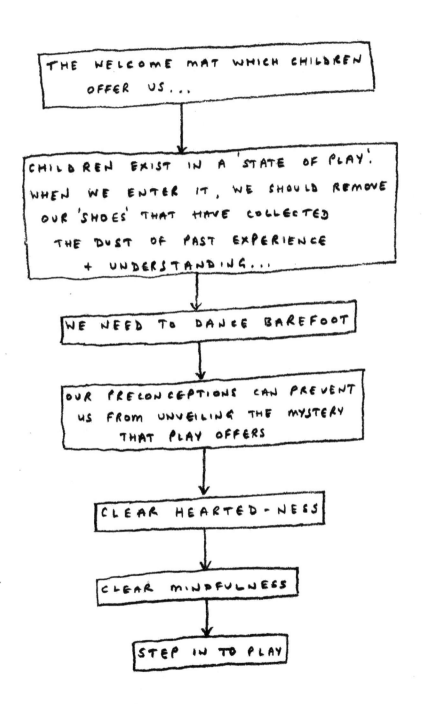

THE WELCOME MAT WHICH CHILDREN OFFER US...

CHILDREN EXIST IN A 'STATE OF PLAY'. WHEN WE ENTER IT, WE SHOULD REMOVE OUR 'SHOES' THAT HAVE COLLECTED THE DUST OF PAST EXPERIENCE + UNDERSTANDING...

WE NEED TO DANCE BAREFOOT

OUR PRECONCEPTIONS CAN PREVENT US FROM UNVEILING THE MYSTERY THAT PLAY OFFERS

CLEAR HEARTED-NESS

CLEAR MINDFULNESS

STEP IN TO PLAY

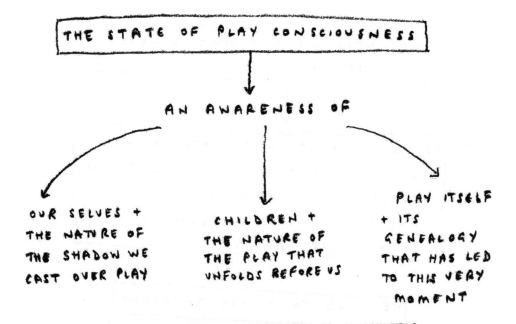

THE STATE OF PLAY CONSCIOUSNESS

AN AWARENESS OF

OUR SELVES + THE NATURE OF THE SHADOW WE CAST OVER PLAY

CHILDREN + THE NATURE OF THE PLAY THAT UNFOLDS BEFORE US

PLAY ITSELF + ITS GENEALOGY THAT HAS LED TO THIS VERY MOMENT

PLAY IS LIKE A STORY PASSED ON FROM GENERATION TO GENERATION

IT IS A STORY TO BE TOLD + RE-TOLD

WHEN WE MAKE SPACE FOR PLAY, WE MAKE SPACE FOR THE PAST TO ECHO INTO THE PRESENT.

WHEN WE OFFER SPACE FOR PLAY THEN WE HONOUR THE PAST.

PLAY IS A PATHWAY FROM THE PAST

IT IS THE BATON OF FREEDOM

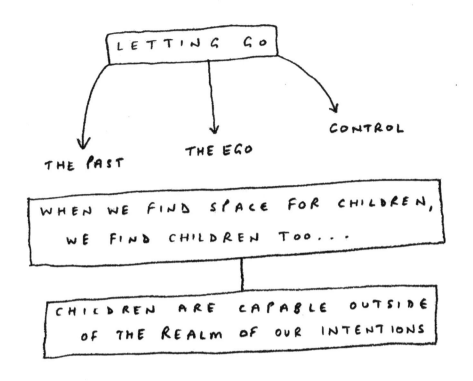

WHEN WE LIBERATE CHILDREN, WE LIBERATE
OURSELVES...

WHAT WE CONTROL, CONTROLS US

WHO WE CONTROL, CONTROLS US

LETTING GO IS TO AWAKEN FROM
THE SLEEPWALK OF THE PAST,
FROM THE 'WHAT-HAS-ALWAYS-BEEN'

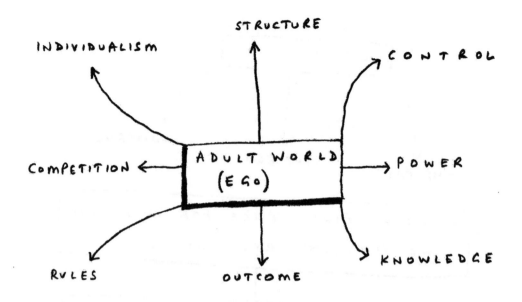

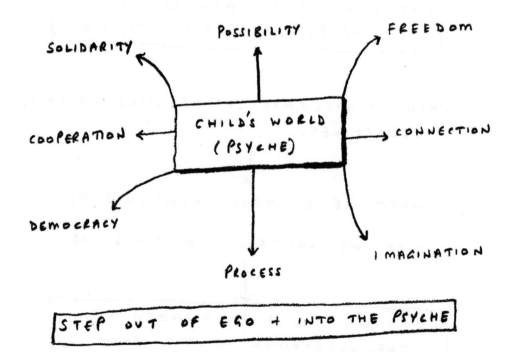

"WHAT IS ESSENTIAL IS TO BE ALIVE +
PRESENT TO ALL THE WONDERS OF LIFE
THAT ARE AVAILABLE..."
                              THICH NHAT HANH

PLAY REVEALS THE ULTIMATE TRUTH
OF LIFE + HOW TO LIVE

TO BE CONSCIOUS, FULLY AWARE IN
THE PRESENT WHERE THE ANXIETIES
OF THE PAST + OF THE FUTURE
NO LONGER TAKE HOLD

WE LOSE OURSELVES IN PLAY
TO FIND OURSELVES AGAIN

CHILDREN STRIP BACK THE VENEERS +
THE MASKS THAT THE ADULT WORLD
PLACES OVER LIFE. THEY REVEAL THE
SIMPLICITY OF LIVING + THAT JOY
IS WITHIN REACH...

THE ACHILLES HEEL OF PLAY

THE ADULT WANTS TRANSPARENCY OF
'DOING-NESS'
THE DEMAND FOR VISIBLE LEARNING

IT SEEKS EVIDENCE FOR ITS
AGENDA

THE LOOK
OF
LEARNING

WHEN WE SHIFT OUR PERSPECTIVE +
BECOME CO-RESEARCHERS, IT IS
THEN THAT WE 'SEE THROUGH' PLAY

WE FIND COOPERATION, CONNECTION
+ THE UNKNOWN - WE NO LONGER
SEEK TO PROVE, INSTEAD WE SEEK
TO DISCOVER...

WE RE-POSITION OURSELVES: WE BECOME
UNKNOWING, WE BECOME UN-SCHOOLED

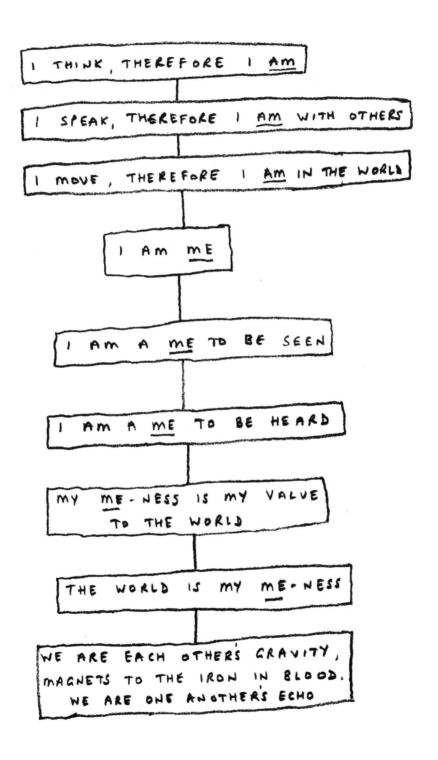

TO GIVE THE GIFT OF PLAY OPENS THE DOOR TO THE ART OF SOUL-SEARCHING

WE ENABLE CHILDREN TO UNRAVEL THEMSELVES UNCONSCIOUSLY + WILLINGLY

CHILDREN SIEZE THE DAY

WHEN CHILDREN PLAY, WE CAN LOOK INTO THEIR SOUL: WE SEE THE SPARK + SENSE LIFE'S POSSIBILITY

PLAY IS AN ACT OF ABANDONMENT

AN ACT OF UNAWARE-NESS

THE UNCONSCIOUSNESS OF PLAY, ITS 'BEING-FOR-ITS-OWN-BEING' BRINGS THE ADULT INTO A NEW CONSCIOUSNESS...

WE BECOME AWARE OF FREEDOM. WE AWAKEN TO LOST MEMORIES, WE 'TIME TRAVEL' BY STEPPING OUT OF OURSELVES + OUR LIMITATIONS: WE SEE LIFE AS A NEW LANDSCAPE.

PLAY IS LIKE AN OUT OF BODY EXPERIENCE

CHILDREN SHOW US THAT ALL IS POSSIBILITY

PLAY IS THE POSSIBILITY OF POSSIBILITIES...

"IN THE HOURS OF IDLE DREAMING..."
THE LILAC TIME

WE NEVER SEEM TO HAVE TIME. WE
SPEND IT. WE WASTE IT. WE SAVE IT.
WE GIVE IT. WE TAKE IT. WE TREAT
TIME LIKE A COMMODITY, LIKE A
CURRENCY...

WE CAN NEVER OWN TIME

WHEN CHILDREN PLAY, THEY SHOW US
THAT BEING TIMELESS IS FAR RICHER

WE NEVER SEEM TO 'FIND TIME':
CHILDREN BRING US TO AN UNDERSTANDING
THAT IT IS FRUITLESS TO LOOK FOR TIME
IN THE FIRST PLACE...

TO BE TIMELESS IS TO FULLY LIVE

PLAY IS A STEP OUT OF TIME

NOT KNOWING WHICH WAY TO TURN...

WHEN CHILDREN PLAY, THEY ENCOUNTER CROSSROADS, ALTERNATIVE PATHWAYS + DIVERSIONS IN BOTH THINKING + DOING.

PLAY IS LIKE AN INFINITE MAZE: IT IS A LABYRINTH TO BE LOST IN

THERE IS NO 'ROUTE'. THERE IS NO PRE-DETERMINATION...

PLAY CAN LEAD ANYWHERE

IT IS AN ACT OF FOLLOWING: WE TAKE THE HAND OF PLAY + ALLOW OURSELVES TO BE LED

PLAY IS FAITH THAT ONE STEP WILL LEAD TO ANOTHER

THE 'MAPLESSNESS' OF PLAY

PLAY IS THE UNKNOWN LANDSCAPE THAT
LIES BEFORE US...

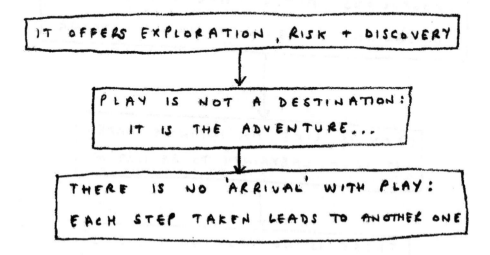

IT OFFERS EXPLORATION, RISK + DISCOVERY

PLAY IS NOT A DESTINATION:
IT IS THE ADVENTURE...

THERE IS NO 'ARRIVAL' WITH PLAY:
EACH STEP TAKEN LEADS TO ANOTHER ONE

WE DON'T GET 'CLOSER TO', BUT WE DO
GET 'FURTHER AWAY' — WE TAKE STEPS
AWAY FROM OURSELVES. WE ENTER
A STATE OF
DEPARTURE-WITHOUT-ARRIVAL

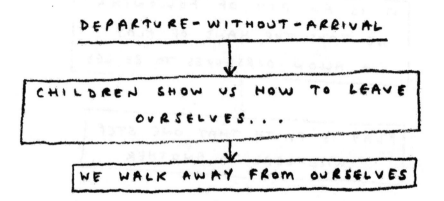

CHILDREN SHOW US HOW TO LEAVE
OURSELVES...

WE WALK AWAY FROM OURSELVES

"TO FIND YOURSELF, THINK FOR YOURSELF..."
SOCRATES

THE SPECIFICS OF YOUR INDIVIDUALITY
- YOU SHOULD BE IRREPLACEABLE

THE UNIQUE PICTURE OF YOU

THINKING - NOT OUTSIDE THE BOX,
BUT RATHER WITH NO BOX AT ALL...

BY FINDING ANSWERS + SOLUTIONS, BY
MAKING SENSE THROUGH PLAY, CHILDREN
FIND THEMSELVES TOO ON THE WAY

CHILDREN CAN THINK FOR THEMSELVES. THEY
MAY HAVE A SOLUTION IN MIND, A HYPOTHESIS,
OR THEY MAY OBSERVE THE STRUGGLE OF
THEIR PEERS + ADAPT TO CREATE NEW
HYPOTHESES...

THROUGH STRUGGLE EMERGES THINKING

IF IT IS THOUGHT FOR ME, IF I HAVE NOT
FACED STRUGGLE THEN I LIVE IN A SHADOW...

OVERCOMING STRUGGLE THROUGH PLAY

"TO CONFRONT A PERSON WITH HIS SHADOW IS TO SHOW HIM HIS OWN LIGHT..." CARL JUNG

PLAY IS THE OPEN SPACE TO TOY WITH STRUGGLE. IT ENABLES CHILDREN TO SEE RISKS + WANT TO OVERCOME THEM. IT PRESENTS FRUSTRATIONS + 'GOING-WRONG-NESS', FALLOUTS + DEFEATS BUT SIMULTANEOUSLY IT OFFERS THE ROUTE TO PATIENCE, TO FRUITION, COOPERATION + CONQUEST...

PLAY CREATES THE EQUANIMITY OF STRUGGLE + ITS OVERCOMING

THROUGH AUTONOMY AND CHOICE, PLAY IS THE FREEDOM TO FAIL + THE POSSIBILITY OF RE-EMERGENCE

STANDING IN THE SHADOW OF FAILURE IS THE SHAPE OF SUCCESS...

THROUGH ADVERSITY AND ITS DEFEAT WE REVEAL OURSELVES TO OURSELVES.

UNSMOOTHING THE PATH

"OUT OF SUFFERING HAVE EMERGED THE STRONGEST SOULS..." KHALIL GIBRAN

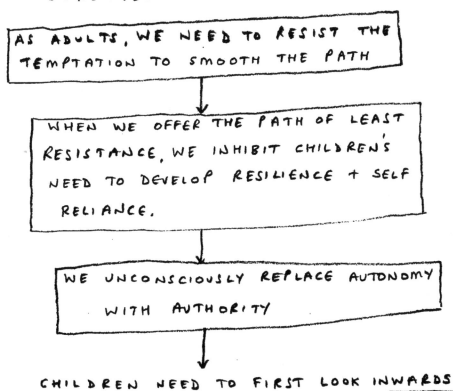

AS ADULTS, WE NEED TO RESIST THE TEMPTATION TO SMOOTH THE PATH

WHEN WE OFFER THE PATH OF LEAST RESISTANCE, WE INHIBIT CHILDREN'S NEED TO DEVELOP RESILIENCE + SELF RELIANCE.

WE UNCONSCIOUSLY REPLACE AUTONOMY WITH AUTHORITY

CHILDREN NEED TO FIRST LOOK INWARDS

DISCOVER STRUGGLE + DEFEAT IT

IF WE ARE TOO QUICK TO SOLVE, EXPLAIN OR COMPLETE FOR CHILDREN, THEN WE BEGIN TO SHAPE CHILDREN WHO LOOK FOR SOLUTIONS OUTSIDE OF THEMSELVES

PLAY + THE ORDER OF THINGS

THE ADULT WORLD SEEKS CONFORMITY. IT VALUES STRUCTURE + LINEARITY. PLAY DEFIES OVERT ORDER. IT HAS AN ORDER OF ITS OWN...

THE TEMPORALITY OF PLAY

PLAY IS AN INFINITE MESH OF IDEAS + ACTIONS. IT IS NOT ALWAYS 'CLEAR'. IT IS DRIVEN BY HIDDEN INTENTIONS

PLAY HAS VALUE FOR ITSELF

THE PSYCHIC STRUCTURE OF PLAY QUIETLY TRANSFORMS CHILDREN. PLAY IS THE SUBTLE ARCHITECT OF THE SELF...

AN ACT OF PLAY MAY SHOW ITSELF BUT MAY NEVER BE SEEN AGAIN. PLAY IS BEYOND 'CONTROL' — IT IS THE FREEDOM OF FREEDOM, IT IS UNCONTAINABILTY.

PLAY FOR TODAY

"WHAT WORRIES YOU, MASTERS YOU..."

JOHN LOCKE

PLAY IS THE JOYFUL EMBRACE OF THE PRESENT.

FEAR FROM THE PAST + ANXIETY FOR THE FUTURE ARE THE INHIBITORS TO LIVING 'PRESENTLY.'...

PLAY IS FULL OF THE PRESENT. IT LOSES CONSCIOUSNESS OF THE PAST + DOES NOT CONCERN ITSELF WITH FUTURE

ADULTS BRING THEIR PAST / FUTURE INTO THE PRESENT-NESS OF CHILDREN.

KNOWLEDGE OF MALEVOLENCE + THE EQUAL ANTICIPATION OF IT, PREVENT ADULTS FROM ACHIEVING 'PLAYFULNESS'...

THE TRANSFERENCE OF FEAR

WE THREATEN TO SHRINK THE WORLD OF ADVENTURE - WE LIMIT THEIR POSSIBILITIES TO OUR OWN

WE PRESENT THE FEAR OF OURSELVES...

THE COLLECTIVISM OF PLAY

INDEPENDENCE ⟵⟶ INTERDEPENDENCE

PLAY OFFERS BOTH INDIVIDUALISM
+ CONNECTIVITY THROUGH COOPERATION

↓

CHILDREN COME TO A POINT IN
PLAY WHEN THEY NEED A HELPING
HAND — TO BECOME 'UNSTUCK'

↓

LOOKING INWARDS THEN OUTWARDS

"I AM CAPABLE TO THIS MOMENT:
I NEED THE CAPABILITY OF OTHERS
TO MOVE FORWARD..."

↓

CHILDREN RECOGNISE THEIR
'WOVEN-NESS' TO OTHER CHILDREN

↓

THE ACCEPTANCE OF LIMITATION
+ THE DESIRE TO GO BEYOND IT

↓

SEEING ONESELF IN THE CONTEXT
OF OTHERS + OTHERNESS

"NOWADAYS PEOPLE KNOW THE PRICE OF
EVERYTHING + THE VALUE OF NOTHING..."

OSCAR WILDE

THE VALUE OF PLAY IS THAT IT SHAPES
A DYNAMIC LIFE, A LIFE OF SHIFTING +
SEARCHING, FINDING, LOSING + FINDING AGAIN.

PLAY IS A DECLARATION OF A LIFE WORTH
LIVING...

PLAY DOESN'T STAND STILL - IT DOESN'T
ROOT CHILDREN TO A SPOT: IT CONTINUALLY
POSES QUESTIONS + SUGGESTS ANSWERS IN
A NEVERENDING CIRCLE OF DISCOVERY...

CHILDREN ARE TRANSPORTED BY PLAY

IT IS A SEARCH FOR THE EVERYTHING
+ THE NOTHING: PLAY IS AN ACT
OF RECOGNISING LIFE FOR WHAT IT
IS, WHAT IT ISN'T + WHAT IT CAN BE

THE ACT OF MAKING SENSE

"A WEIRD TIME IN WHICH WE ARE ALIVE. WE CAN TRAVEL ANYWHERE WE WANT, EVEN TO OTHER PLANETS. AND FOR WHAT? TO SIT DAY AFTER DAY, DECLINING IN MORALE + HOPE."

PHILIP K DICK

PLAY IS HOPE

HOPE FOR A NEW INTERPRETATION OF THE WORLD. HOPE FOR IMAGINATION + EXPLORATION + DREAM. PLAY IS BURSTING WITH HOPE...

PLAY ENERGISES US TO BELIEVE

IT IS THE FOUNDATION OF FAITH IN A NEW FUTURE OF CAPABILITY, CREATIVY + CONFIDENCE

PLAY'S ACCESSIBILITY FOR CHILDREN, ITS SOLIDARITY + ACCEPTANCE OFFERS HOPE FOR ALL

WHEN YOU HAVE A DREAM, YOU WAKE UP...

PLAY KEEPS YOU DIFFERENT

IT IS YOUR UNIQUE TAKE ON THE WORLD, YOUR EXPRESSION OF YOUR 'YOU-NESS' + THE ADVENTURE YOU ARE CAPABLE OF HAVING IN THE WORLD

↓

HOLD ON TO DIFFERENCE

↓

PLAY 'SINGLES YOU OUT'

↓

PLAY IS THE LANDSCAPE OF IDENTITY, OF YOUR ORIGINALITY - IT TELLS THE WORLD WHO YOU ARE...

↓

PLAY IDENTIFIES YOU + THROUGH YOUR ACTIONS + THINKING OTHERS ACKNOWLEDGE + MIRROR THE JOY OF KNOWING ONESELF

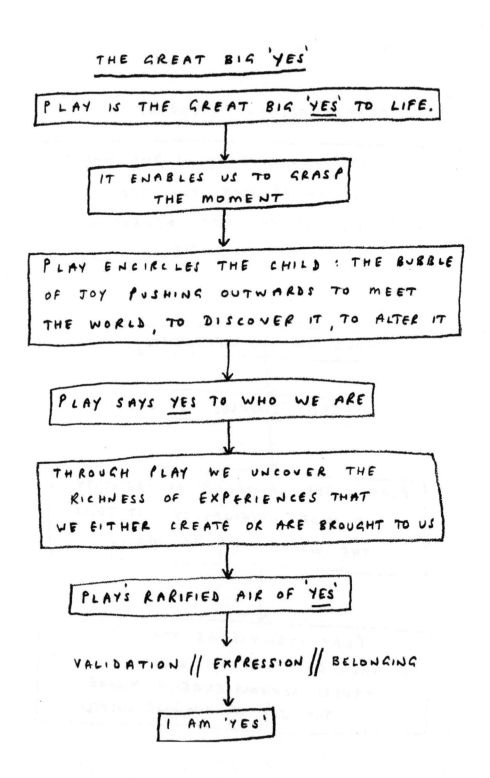

THE GREAT BIG 'YES'

PLAY IS THE GREAT BIG 'YES' TO LIFE.

IT ENABLES US TO GRASP THE MOMENT

PLAY ENCIRCLES THE CHILD : THE BUBBLE OF JOY PUSHING OUTWARDS TO MEET THE WORLD, TO DISCOVER IT, TO ALTER IT

PLAY SAYS YES TO WHO WE ARE

THROUGH PLAY WE UNCOVER THE RICHNESS OF EXPERIENCES THAT WE EITHER CREATE OR ARE BROUGHT TO US

PLAY'S RARIFIED AIR OF 'YES'

VALIDATION // EXPRESSION // BELONGING

I AM 'YES'

"THE REAL VOYAGE OF DISCOVERY CONSISTS NOT IN SEEKING NEW LANDSCAPES, BUT IN HAVING NEW EYES." MARCEL PROUST

TO SEE THE POETRY OF PLAY WE NEED A NEW PERSPECTIVE, ONE THAT VALUES THE INTRINSIC POWER OF COLLABORATION + COOPERATION, ONE THAT RECOGNISES LIFE BEYOND CURRICULUM, BEYOND CONTROL...

TO SEE THE UNLOOKED-FOR TO 'SEE THE UNSEEN'

LOOKING THROUGH THE LENS OF LOVE

THE MORE WE LOOK, THE MORE WE LOVE; THE MORE WE LOVE, THE MORE WE LOOK.

LETTING GO OF PERCEPTIONS LETTING GO OF SUBJUGATION...

THE EXPLOSIONS OF PLAY

WHEN PLAY REVEALS ITSELF, WHEN IT SHOWS US THE SOUL OF CHILDREN, IT CAN BE LIKE FIREWORKS IN THE NIGHT SKY...

THE UNEXPECTED COLOURS OF PLAY

PLAY HAS THE ABILITY TO SHOCK OUR SYSTEMS

IT HAS THE ELEMENT OF SURPRISE

THE CONSCIOUSNESS OF CAPABILITY + CREATIVITY

A FLASH OF PLAY CAN LEAD US TO ANTICIPATION + WONDER

WHAT IS POSSIBLE?

THE SILENCE + THE SOUND OF PLAY

PLAY CAN TAKE MANY FORMS. IT CAN
BE THE BUZZ OF THE CROWD, OF
EXCITED COLLUSION + INTER-PARTICIPATION;
IT CAN BE THE TO-AND-FRO OF TWO OR
THREE EVOLVING AN IDEA OR 'STORY'; OR
IT CAN BE THE QUIETNESS OF SOLITUDE,
THE INTERNAL DIALOGUE, PENSIVE MOMENTS
OF PONDERING + THINKING WITHIN ...

EACH ACT OF PLAY HAS UNIQUE VALUE

THE DYNAMICS OF PLAY MEAN
THAT THE VOLUME OF SOUND CAN
EVOLVE IN ACCORDANCE WITH WHAT IS
BEING DISCOVERED + HOW...

INTERCHANGEABLE SOUNDSCAPE

THE RIPPLE EFFECT

PLAY CARRIES WITH IT A LAW OF ATTRACTION. IT HAS THE UNSPOKEN ABILITY TO DRAW CHILDREN TO IT...

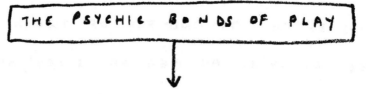

THE PSYCHIC BONDS OF PLAY

↓

THE ENERGY OF PLAY IS AN INVITATION TO JOIN IN, TO EVOLVE ALONGSIDE ONE ANOTHER...

↓

COLLABORATION IS ADDITION: EACH NEW PARTICIPANT BRINGS WITH THEM THE POTENTIAL TO LEVEL UP

↓

PLAY UNFOLDS OUTWARDS

↓

A CATHEDRAL OF IDEA + ACTION

MIND READING

PLAY ENABLES THE DEVELOPMENT OF THE BODY + THE EXPANSION OF THE MIND...

↓

EDUCATORS AS MIND READERS DELVING INTO UNDERSTANDING THROUGH A PROCESS OF COMBINING PRIOR KNOWLEDGE, GUESSWORK + CONNECTION

↓

WE BECOME PLAY DETECTIVES

↓

PIECING CLUES TOGETHER + UNEARTHING EVIDENCE + COMING INTO KNOWLEDGE

↓

THE DISCOVERY OF MYSTERY

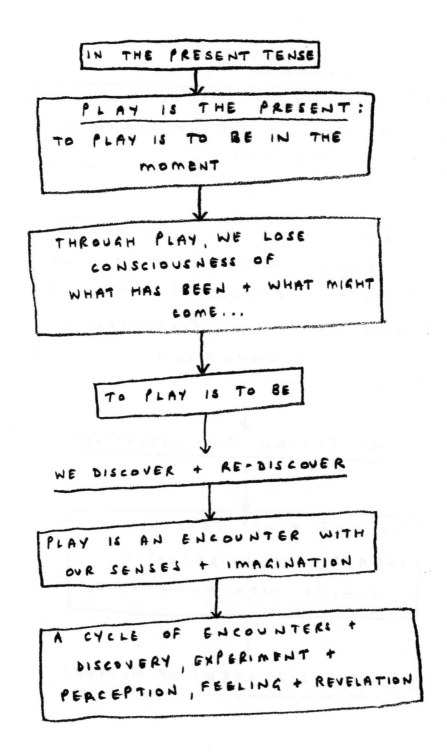

IN THE PRESENT TENSE

PLAY IS THE PRESENT:
TO PLAY IS TO BE IN THE
MOMENT

THROUGH PLAY, WE LOSE
CONSCIOUSNESS OF
WHAT HAS BEEN + WHAT MIGHT
COME...

TO PLAY IS TO BE

WE DISCOVER + RE-DISCOVER

PLAY IS AN ENCOUNTER WITH
OUR SENSES + IMAGINATION

A CYCLE OF ENCOUNTERS +
DISCOVERY, EXPERIMENT +
PERCEPTION, FEELING + REVELATION

THE STRENGTH OF KINDNESS

YOU CAN'T LOVE EVERYONE, BUT YOU CAN BE KIND TO THEM...

PERHAPS THIS MEANS THAT KINDNESS IS GREATER THAN LOVE? OR IF NOT, THEN IT IS A DILUTED VERSION OF LOVE SO CAN GO FURTHER?

PLAY IS KINDNESS: WELCOMING, ACCEPTANCE, CARE, TEAMWORK, PATIENCE, ENABLEMENT, SHARING, VALIDATION

PLAY IS AN EXPRESSION OF KINDNESS, OF 'SEEING-NESS'

PLAY REVEALS MORALITY OF CAUSE + EFFECT...

THE GO BETWEEN

THE ADULT'S ROLE IS TO ACT AS A MESSENGER FROM THE WORLD OF SKILLS + TO ENTER CHILDREN'S PLAY WITH SENSITIVITY, TO SPRINKLE THEM OVER THE BEING-NESS OF CHILDREN + THE DOING-NESS THEY PRESENT TO US

WE CARRY A 'MESSAGE' FROM THE ADULT WORLD, BUT WE NEED TO RETURN WITH A NEW MESSAGE TOO...

THE BACK + FORTH OF THE GO-BETWEEN...

THE MESSAGE IS TWO-WAY! THIS IS ME ⟶ THIS IS YOU...

THE MESSAGE BACK FROM CHILDREN SHOULD HAVE MORE VALUE FOR THE GO-BETWEEN

PERPETUAL MOTION

PLAY IS CONSTANT

IT HAS DIVERGENT FORMS:
WHAT APPEARS AS CHAOS HAS
A RHYTHM + A NATURAL ORDER
BENEATH IT

THE POWER OF PLAY LIES
IN ITS ABILITY TO MOVE CHILDREN
FORWARD IN ITS RHYTHM...

PLAY MOVES CHILDREN FORWARD BUT
IT CAN TAKE ANY DIRECTION

THE DANCING MOVEMENT OF PLAY
ENABLES CHILDREN TO ENCOUNTER DISCORD
+ DIFFICULTY - RATHER THAN AVOID
THEM, CHILDREN DANCE WITH THEM TOO

"THERE'S NOWHERE ELSE I'D RATHER BE..."

THIS IS THE MESSAGE OF PLAY
TO THE ADULT WORLD

PLAY IS A SIGNAL OF
CONTENTMENT, OF BEING
IN THE ARMS OF THE MOMENT...

IF I WANTED TO BE SOMEWHERE ELSE
THEN I WOULD BE...

PLAY IS THE HAPPINESS OF
BEING IN A PARTICULAR
TIME + PLACE

THE PERFECT MOMENT IN TIME

WHERE PLAY LIVES THEN SO DO
CHILDREN...

"ALL THAT IS OUTSIDE, ALSO IS INSIDE..."

CARL JUNG

PERCEPTION

EXPERIENCE

PLAY IS CHILDREN'S WAY OF <u>FEELING</u> THE WORLD. IT IS THEIR ROUTE TO CREATING MEANING OF + FOR THEMSELVES.

<u>PERCEPTION OF SELF, PERCEPTION OF OTHER</u>

THROUGH PLAY, CHILDREN ARRIVE AT THE CUSP OF THEIR LIMITATIONS, THEY DISCOVER THE PARAMETERS OF WHAT THEY ARE CAPABLE OF + MORE IMPORTANTLY, HOW TO GO BEYOND THEM + INTO THE NEW...

PLAY ENABLES NEW PERCEPTIONS + THE POSSIBILITY THAT LIFE CAN BE RE-IMAGINED + SEEN OUTSIDE OF WHAT IS PRESENTED BY ONE'S CULTURE

<u>PLAY IS THE VOICE OF THE HUMAN SPIRIT</u>

CREATION BEGINS TODAY

WHEN WE VALUE CHILDREN'S CONSTRUCTIVE ART, WHEN WE RECOGNISE THE FORMING OF SOMETHING FROM THE MIND BEFORE US WITH ALL ITS STUGGLE + THE OVERCOMING OF IT, WHEN WE SEE THAT SOMETHING HAS BEEN BROUGHT INTO EXISTENCE WITH CARE + PURPOSE, WE GLIMPSE THE REAL MEANING OF 'CREATIVITY'.

SOMETHING FROM DEEP WITHIN

THE ACT OF EMERGENCE

CREATIVITY HAS INTRINSIC VALUE FOR THE CHILD. IT IS OUR ROLE NOT TO QUESTION OR ALTER IT BUT TO SEE IT THROUGH EYES THAT HAVE BEEN THERE TOO, HAVE EXPERIENCED THE URGE OF CHILDHOOD TO BRING SOMETHING INTO THE WORLD WITH A 'PIECE OF THEM' IN IT...

IMPULSE + INSTINCT

PLAY EXISTS ON THE HORIZON OF IMPULSE + REFLECTION. IT IS A DRIVE TO MEET THE WORLD HEAD ON TEMPERED BY THE GROWTH OF UNDERSTANDING + THINKINGNESS.

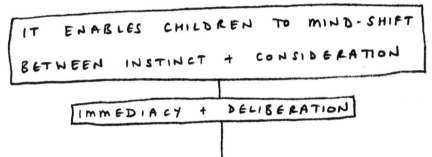

IT ENABLES CHILDREN TO MIND-SHIFT BETWEEN INSTINCT + CONSIDERATION

IMMEDIACY + DELIBERATION

WHEN PLAY HAPPENS, TWO WEATHER FRONTS COME TOGETHER : THE SQUALL OF URGENCY, THE URGE TO THROW ONESELF IN, MEETING THE REPOSE OF TAKING STOCK, THE KNOWLEDGE OF TAKING A STEP BACK TO SURVEY THE VIEW...

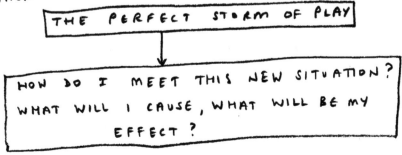

THE PERFECT STORM OF PLAY

HOW DO I MEET THIS NEW SITUATION? WHAT WILL I CAUSE, WHAT WILL BE MY EFFECT ?

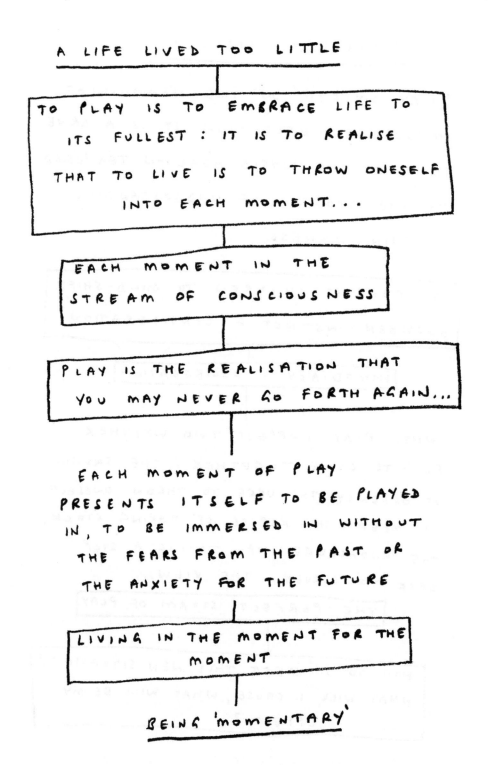

A LIFE LIVED TOO LITTLE

TO PLAY IS TO EMBRACE LIFE TO ITS FULLEST : IT IS TO REALISE THAT TO LIVE IS TO THROW ONESELF INTO EACH MOMENT...

EACH MOMENT IN THE STREAM OF CONSCIOUSNESS

PLAY IS THE REALISATION THAT YOU MAY NEVER GO FORTH AGAIN...

EACH MOMENT OF PLAY PRESENTS ITSELF TO BE PLAYED IN, TO BE IMMERSED IN WITHOUT THE FEARS FROM THE PAST OR THE ANXIETY FOR THE FUTURE

LIVING IN THE MOMENT FOR THE MOMENT

BEING 'MOMENTARY'

LIFE IS TOO SHORT TO BE NORMAL...

PLAY IS NOT CONFORMITY. IT ISN'T 'FITTING-IN-NESS'. IT ISN'T CONVENTION OR CONTROL. PLAY ISN'T DOCILE : IT IS POWER. IT ISN'T ACQUIESCENCE : IT IS FREEDOM. PLAY IS ALLEGIANCE TO ONESELF + ONE'S PEERS, NOT RESIGNATION...

THERE IS NO ORTHODOXY IN PLAY, NO ASSENT TO VOICES OUTSIDE OF ITSELF

PLAY OBSERVES ITS OWN PREROGATIVE

PLAY'S NATURE IS ONE OF DEFIANCE

IT HAS NO 'NORMALITY' INSTEAD, IT HAS MYSTERY, A COMPLEX SIMPLICITY, LAYERS TO PEEL AWAY TO DISCOVER FURTHER LAYERS LIKE AN INTRICATE PUZZLE - A WEB OF UNCERTAINTY + PERPLEXITY...

"I CAN'T UNDERSTAND WHY PEOPLE ARE
FRIGHTENED OF NEW IDEAS. I'M FRIGHTENED
OF THE OLD ONES..." JOHN CAGE

THE NEW IDEAS OF PLAY

PLAY IS INVENTION + RE-INVENTION

IT INVENTS NEW CREATIONS,
NEW CONNECTIONS, NEW EXPLORATIONS

IT RE-INVENTS WHAT HAS GONE
BEFORE; IT IS RE-IMAGINATION,
A SENSE OF THE PAST BEING
RE-CONDITIONED...

PLAY IS A CONSTANT
STATE OF RENEWAL

THE REGENERATION OF PLAY

"HAVE YOU EVER STARTED A PATH? NO ONE SEEMS WILLING TO DO THIS. WE DON'T MIND EXISTING PATHS, BUT WE RARELY START NEW ONES. DO IT TODAY, START A PATH, EVEN IF IT DOESN'T LEAD ANYWHERE..."

GEORGE CARLIN

THE 'DO-IT-TODAY' OF PLAY

PLAY IS A NEW PATH.
IT DOESN'T HAVE TO LEAD ANYWHERE.
IT IS A PATH FOR ITS OWN DELIGHT...

PLAY IS A PATH TO ITSELF BUT ALSO TO THE ENDLESS POSSIBILITIES OF EXPLORATION + ADVENTURE

WHEN WE ENABLE PLAY WE ARE ENABLING THE BEGINNING NOT JUST ONE PATH, BUT INFINITE

THE LAUGHTER OF PLAY

THE JOY OF PLAY IS INFECTIOUS,
IT'S LIKE A YAWN SPREADING ACROSS
A CROWDED ROOM.

DELIGHT BRINGS US TOWARDS ONE
ANOTHER LIKE MAGNETS...

JOY IS CONNECTIVITY –
IT BECOMES A SHARED MOMENT
WHERE THE LAUGHTER + THE
SENSE OF LIFE LIVED SPILLS OUT
OF US FOR ALL TO SEE + SHARE IN

THE JOY OF PLAY IS AT THE
HEART OF ITS SOLIDARITY

A NEVERENDING PASS THE PARCEL

THE SHARING OF THE JOY OF PLAY
IS THE SHARING OF HOPE

BEING CONTENT TO GET NOWHERE

"WE DON'T SEE THINGS AS THEY ARE,
WE SEE THEM AS WE ARE..." ANAIS NIN

THE ADULT WORLD WANTS CHILDREN TO GET THE MILESTONES IT HAS DECIDED FOR THEM IN THE TIMEFRAME IT HAS DECIDED FOR THEM TOO...

THE ADULT WORLD ALSO WANTS TO DECIDE THE 'HOW'

IT WANTS TO SPEED LIFE UP + GO AGAINST THE GRAIN OF PLAY

YET THE ADULT WORLD COULD CHANGE ITS AGENDA + EMBRACE THE FLOW OF PLAY

WHEN WE SEE THAT VALUING PLAY IS A CHOICE, THEN HOPE EXISTS THAT IT CAN + WILL BE MADE...

MAKING MEMORIES

CHILDHOOD ISN'T ABOUT NOSTALGIA OR A 'GOLDEN AGE' OF INNOCENCE. IT'S THE LANDSCAPE OF MEMORY, OF EXPERIENCES + HOW WE LEARN TO PERCEIVE + RESPOND TO THEM.

IT IS THE PLAYGROUND OF THE MIND

EVERY EXPERIENCE + THE ABILITY TO REACT OR ACT WITHIN THEM SHAPES EACH CHILD'S 'ME-NESS'...

THE AUTONOMY TO SELECT OUR OWN COURSE OF ACTION + THE FREEDOM TO 'MAKE SOMETHING' OF OURSELVES...

THE MEMORY OF WHAT WENT BEFORE, OUR RECOLLECTION OF THE IMMEDIATE PAST ENABLES US TO DISCOVER THE PASSAGE THROUGH ADVERSITY...

A DISCOVERY OF OURSELVES, FOR OURSELVES...

AUTHORITY OR AUTONOMY?

> WHEN DECISIONS ARE MADE FOR CHILDREN, WHEN THE DAY-SHAPE IS PRE-DETEMINED, WHEN THE ADULT WORLD HOLDS THE POWER OF DO-THIS-BECAUSE-I-TOLD-YOU-TO, THEN THEY ARE DIMINISHED BEFORE OUR VERY EYES...

↓

AUTHORITY REPLACES THE POSSIBILITY OF SELF-DETERMINATION

↓

> AUTHORITY CLOSES DOWN CHOICE + THE ABILITY TO SEE ONE'S FREEDOM

↓

AUTONOMY FOR CHILDREN OPENS UP DOORS TO THE SELF:
- RESILIENCE
- PATIENCE
- SELECTION
- COURAGE
- DECIDING
- RESPONSIBILITY

> THE AUTONOMY IN PLAY IS AN ACT OF SELF-SELECTION...

THE WHISPER OF PLAY

PLAY IS LIKE A TINY VOICE IN EACH CHILD'S EAR, ENCOURAGING, QUESTIONING, PROMPTING, ASSESSING, CHALLENGING + ENCHANTING...

THE WHISPER OF PLAY CALLS CHILDREN ON...

IT BECKONS THEM INTO EXPLORATION + ADVENTURE

CHILDREN BECOME THE ECHO CHAMBER OF PLAY - AMPLIFYING THE JOY OF DISCOVERY + SELF-FULFILMENT...

THROUGH CHILDREN, PLAY MAKES LIFE BECOME KNOWN

THE PRESENCE OF PLAY IS THE PRESENCE OF LIFE

THE LAND OF THE RISING SUN

WHEN PLAY EMERGES + TAKES ROOT
IT LETS IN THE LIGHT.
WE SEE CHILDREN FOR WHO THEY ARE
+ WHAT THEY ARE CAPABLE OF IN
THE FUTURE...

THE LIGHTNESS OF PLAY IS THE
LIGHTNESS OF BEING...

WE DON'T HIDE CHILDREN:
WE REVEAL THEM

EACH CHILD ADDS THEIR INDIVIDUAL
LITTLE LIGHTS UNTIL PLAY
BECOMES A CONSTELLATION:
WE LOOK IN WONDER...

THE LIGHTS OF PLAY + CHILDREN
REFLECT ONE ANOTHER: THE
GOLDEN LIGHT

TAKE COURAGE

LIFE PRESENTS STRUGGLE + ADVERSITY.
PLAY PRESENTS THE TOOLS TO DISCOVER
THE WAY OF STRUGGLE + THE COURAGE TO
OVERCOME IT...

THE ADULT WORLD'S ROLE IS TO CREATE
THE CONDITIONS FOR CHILDREN TO
ENCOUNTER STRUGGLE FOR THEMSELVES
+ DEVELOP THE 'RIGHT THINKING' TO FIND
A WAY THROUGH IT...

WHEN WE ENABLE PLAY, WE ENABLE STRUGGLE

OUR ROLE IS NOT TO ADD STRUGGLE
BUT TO UNVEIL IT

WE ENABLE CHILDREN TO TAKE
COURAGE + MOVE FORWARD...

PLAY IS THE INTERPLAY OF
HARDSHIP + SUCCESS

DEPTHS + SURFACE

THE CONDITIONING OF THE ADULT WORLD LEADS IT TO LOOK AT SURFACE, AT THE VENEER OF WHAT IT SEES. IT WANTS IMMEDIACY, THE OBVIOUS, THE CLEAR-TO-SEE.

PLAY HAS AN UNSEEN DEPTH. IT DEFIES THE DESIRE FOR IMMEDIATE CLARITY WITH ITS COMPLEXITY...

PLAY NEEDS THE ADULT WORLD TO FIND TIME TO LOOK DEEPER, TO LOOK BEYOND

PLAY REQUIRES A NEW PERCEPTION IT DEMANDS A NEW VISION

TO EXPLORE WHAT LIES BENEATH

THE HIDDEN WORLD OF PLAY

LIFE WANTS TO BE REAL

CHILDREN MEET LIFE AUTHENTICALLY
- THE ART OF 'NO-MASK'

THEY WISH TO LIVE IT FOR
THEMSELVES...

THE SAFETY OF PLAY TO EXPLORE PERSONA

THE UNMASKING OF THE SELF
IS ONLY POSSIBLE IN THE ACT OF
PLAY...

SELF-NESS

PLAY IS THE VISIBILITY OF
THE SELF; THE FORMED
+ THE NOT-YET-FORMED

MAY EACH GO THEIR OWN WAY

PLAY IS POSSIBILITY NOT PREDETERMINATION

THE WAY OF PLAY IS NOT ALWAYS
EXPLICIT : IT DOES NOT STAND BEFORE
US

PLAY UNWRAPS ITSELF
ACROSS EACH POINT IN TIME
OFFERING DIVERSIONS + ALTERNATIVES

THE WAY CAN BE A SOLO-JOURNEY
OR IT COULD BE THE THRONG
OF COLLABORATION +
COOPERATION

IT HAS NO FIXED IDENTITY

PLAY IS THE FREEDOM OF MOVEMENT

PLAY IS THE FREEDOM TO CHOOSE ONE'S OWN
PATH : THE FREEDOM TO DRAW ONE'S OWN MAP

BEING WHO YOU WILL BECOME

PLAY IS THE POSSIBILITY OF BEING YOUR FUTURE SELF BY BEING IN THE PRESENT. IT CONTAINS ALL THE NUTRIENTS TO MOVE FORWARD WITH.

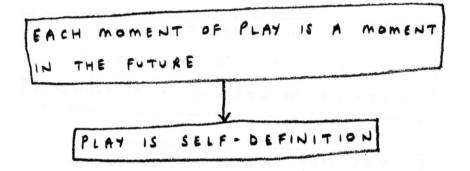

EACH MOMENT OF PLAY IS A MOMENT IN THE FUTURE

PLAY IS SELF-DEFINITION

IT IS NOT ABOUT WHAT YOU WILL BECOME. PLAY IS ABOUT WHO YOU ARE NOW + WHO YOU WILL BECOME...

THE CLAY OF PLAY

CHILDREN MOULD THEMSELVES IN PLAY THE ACT OF SELF-MASTERY...

THE LONGING FOR LIGHT

EACH OF US SEEKS JOY, THOSE MOMENTS, HOWEVER BRIEF, WHEN WE ENTER A STATE OF 'LETTING-GO-NESS' + FIND OURSELVES MOVED OUTSIDE OF TIME. SUCH MOMENTS CAN SEEM LIKE THEY SHRINK AWAY AS WE GROW OLDER, YET CHILDREN WHEN THEY PLAY REMIND US THAT JOY IS ALWAYS IN REACH, THAT LIFE AWAITS IF WE WOULD JUST PUT OUT OUR HANDS + BE...

WE LOOK TOWARDS THE LIGHT

THE LIGHT OF PLAY, THE LIGHT OF BEING...

PLAY IS A SIGNPOST TOWARDS THE POSSIBILITY OF JOY...

PLAY IS THE LIGHT OF LOVE, OF TRANSFORMATION, OF LIVING FULLY WITH THE HEART + AN OPEN MIND

LOOKING BACKWARDS + FORWARDS

CHILDREN ARE PROGRAMMED TO PLAY

PLAY WAITS FOR CHILDREN WITH OPEN ARMS

WHEN THE ADULT WORLD OPENS ITS EYES TO THE VALUE + INTRICACIES OF PLAY, THEN IT SEES ITS OWN CHILDHOOD

WE DON'T GROW OUT OF PLAY : WE ARE TOLD THAT WE HAVE...

WE NEVER TRULY STOP THE URGE TO PLAY - IT IS ETERNAL

BY LOOKING BACK TO OUR OWN CHILDHOOD WE CAN FEEL THE ECHO OF PLAY - WE SENSE ITS POWER, ITS CALL

BY LOOKING BACKWARDS
WE ARE LOOKING FORWARDS:
WE SEE 'NOT-GROWING-OUT-NESS'...

MEMORY + EXPECTATION

PLAY ENABLES CHILDREN TO REACH BACK INTO PAST EXPERIENCE + MEET THE PRESENT WITH SOLUTIONS + THINKINGNESS

DISCOVERIES FROM THE PAST CAN BE RE-IMAGINED + TESTED

THE ADAPTABILITY OF THE PAST

CREATION OF THE PRESENT

EMERGENCE OF THE FUTURE

THE 'POSITIVE MEMORY' OF PLAY

EXPECTATIONS BASED ON MEMORY: THE SPARK TO ADVENTURE...

MEMORIES TRAIL BEHIND ME, EXPECTATIONS PULL US ON...

MAKING SPACES

PLAY IS THE EXPLORATION OF SPACE

WIDE
OPEN

NARROW

INNER

PLAY EMBRACES THE BIG, WIDE WORLD:
RUNNING, JUMPING, CLIMBING, CRAWLING
ALL EXPLORING THE WHAT-IFS OF THE
BODY IN ITS ENVIRONMENT

THE JOY OF OPEN SPACES

PLAY SIMILARLY COMPELLS CHILDREN TO
HIDE, BURROW, SQUEEZE, CONFINE THEMSELVES
INTO THE COSY NARROWNESS OF
DENS + HIDEY-HOLES...

THROW OURSELVES INTO THE WORLD OR RETREAT
FROM IT

CHILDREN MAKE SPACES WORK FOR THEM
THROUGH SENSORY CONNECTION WHICH IN
TURN OPENS THE INNER SPACE OF IMAGINATION
+ THE EMERGENCE OF INDIVIDUALITY...

"IT TAKES COURAGE TO GROW UP
+ BECOME WHO YOU REALLY ARE..."

E. E. CUMMINGS

PLAY IS COURAGE: COURAGE TO BELIEVE;
TO RISK; TO LOSE; TO CONFRONT THE
WORLD; TO SHARE DREAMS; TO THROW
ONESELF INTO LIFE + TO FEEL THE
JOY UNDER THE SKIN...

PLAY IS THE COURAGE OF SELF

IT IS THE STRENGTH TO SEARCH OUTSIDE
OF ONESELF TO DISCOVER NEW DREAMS

EACH NEW DREAM, EACH NEW PIECE OF
LIFE CHILDREN BRING TO LIGHT THROUGH
THE ACT OF PLAY, OFFERS A WINDOW
TO LOOK THROUGH: TO SEE WHO WE
REALLY ARE + WHO WE ARE BECOMING

PLAY IS THE BECOMING OF OURSELVES...

QUESTION EVERYTHING

```
┌──────────────────────────────────────────┐
│ PLAY IS THE GREAT BIG 'WHY?' + THE        │
│ GREAT BIG 'HOW?'                          │
└──────────────────────────────────────────┘
                    │
                    ▼
┌──────────────────────────────────────────┐
│ PLAY FINDS NEW ANSWERS TO                 │
│ EVERY QUESTION...                         │
└──────────────────────────────────────────┘
                    │
                    ▼
┌──────────────────────────────────────────┐
│ THE ADULT WORLD DEMANDS MEMORISATION,     │
│ CONFORMITY + LINEARITY...                 │
└──────────────────────────────────────────┘
                    │
                    ▼
┌──────────────────────────────────────────┐
│ THE ADULT WORLD WANTS IMMEDIATE           │
│ ANSWERS                                   │
└──────────────────────────────────────────┘
                    │
                    ▼
┌──────────────────────────────────────────┐
│ PLAY SAYS 'NO' - IT GIVES PERMISSION      │
│ TO FAIL, TO CONTINUING LOOKING,           │
│ TO SEARCH FOR THE ANSWERS                 │
└──────────────────────────────────────────┘
                    │
                    ▼
┌──────────────────────────────────────────┐
│ RAISING QUESTIONS NOT ALWAYS              │
│ ANSWERING THEM                            │
└──────────────────────────────────────────┘
                    │
                    ▼
┌──────────────────────────────────────────┐
│ PLAY TEACHES THE HUMILITY TO LET GO       │
│ OF THE AUTHORITY OF 'ANSWER'...           │
└──────────────────────────────────────────┘
                    │
                    ▼
┌──────────────────────────────────────────┐
│ PLAY IS AN OPEN QUESTION...               │
└──────────────────────────────────────────┘
```

THE SANCTUARY OF PLAY

IN 'ALONE' PLAY, CHILDREN FIND THE SOLACE OF IMAGINATION + THE 'VOICE' OF BEING-BY-MYSELF...

PLAY CAN SERVE TO DISCONNECT CHILDREN FROM THE WORLD: THEY CAN UNHITCH FROM THE RUSH

THROUGH QUIET PLAY, CHILDREN FIND SPACE TO LISTEN TO THE INNER VOICE

IT ENABLES CHILDREN TO TURN THEIR PERCEPTIONS OF THE WORLD OVER IN THEIR MINDS

THE RETREAT OF PLAY

TO LOOK WITHIN IN THE MOMENTS OF SECLUSION ENABLES US TO LOOK OUTSIDE OURSELVES IN THE MOMENTS OF SOCIAL-NESS... THIS IS MY VOICE IN THE CROWD